Commune
on the
Frontier

Women of America
MILTON MELTZER, EDITOR

Commune
on the
Frontier
The Story of FRANCES
WRIGHT

By Richard Stiller
Illustrated with Photographs

THOMAS Y. CROWELL COMPANY   NEW YORK

W
JB
HT

DESIGNED BY JILL SCHWARTZ

Manufactured in the United States of America

L.C. Card 79-187946   ISBN 0-690-20401-9
1 2 3 4 5 6 7 8 9 10

Acknowledgments

ALTHOUGH Frances Wright wrote a great many letters (sometimes two and three in one day, some of them many pages in length), not many have survived. Those that are to be found scattered in various collections are not always typical of her bright and breezy private pen, so different from the more formal prose style of her public writings.

It was my extremely good fortune to meet Cecilia Payne Gaposchkin, a Harvard astronomer and great-granddaughter of one of Frances Wright's closest friends. Mrs. Gaposchkin has in her possession a great many unpublished letters written by and about Frances Wright and her sister, Camilla. She has kindly made these available to me, and for this I am deeply grateful to her.

I am also grateful to Phoebe Harvey, great-granddaughter of Frances Wright, for permission to quote from these and other letters.

Two other individuals have also been extremely helpful: Miriam Holden, whose extensive private collection of books and papers on the woman's rights movements includes rare editions of Frances Wright's earliest books; and Nancy Woloch, whose parallel research turned up some letters I had been unable to find.

There are Frances Wright papers in a number of libraries, but the collection of the Public Library of Cincinnati and Hamilton County holds the most important of these. I am especially indebted to Yeatman Anderson III, curator of special collections, for his help in finding these and for permission to quote from them. Other collections that have permitted quotation from unpublished manuscripts are the Cincinnati Historical Society, the Historical Society of Pennsylvania, the New York-Historical Society, the Library of the University of Chicago, and the British Museum. I am grateful to them.

The Schomburg Collection in New York City was of help as a source of information about the lives of black people in New York in the early 1800's and about the arrangement between the government of Haiti and American abolitionists by which some blacks were able to emigrate as free men to that island.

For help in translating certain letters from the French, I wish to thank Lyn Birenbaum, Jack Segura, and Marguerite and Burhan Juka. For her skillful typing of the manuscript, I am grateful to Sylvia Shelton.

Fanny Licht Stiller combined her sharp editorial criticisms with her usual warm encouragement. For these I thank her.

Richard Stiller

In Memory
of
Rose Russell

The mind has no sex.

FRANCES WRIGHT

Contents

I
The Making of a Philosopher

Think for yourself, or you may hear and read all the thoughts that ever were spoken and be a fool at last.

FRANCES WRIGHT

Chapter 1 THE RIGHT TO THINK

"Ask why!"

FRANCES WRIGHT

As she stood on the lecture platform, everything about Frances Wright said, *I am my own master. My thoughts are free.*

She was very tall for a woman, taller than many men, as straight and slim as a Lombardy poplar. She had warm chestnut-brown hair; its curls softened her strong face.

Her eyes were deep and blue and far apart. They looked straight ahead with a directness not often found in a young woman. People who did not like her opinions said she had a masculine look.

The crowd in the Cincinnati courthouse watched and waited with quiet, polite impatience. There was no room to walk about; the aisles were filled with people. Standees pressed against the wall at the back. Five hundred latecomers stood outside, unable to get in, straining to hear every scrap of sound that filtered through the open windows.

Half the audience were women and girls—an unusual sight. Women did not ordinarily go to public meetings in 1828, unless they were church meetings. What was even more unusual was the woman herself, standing on the platform, about to deliver a lecture. If the crowd had come to see, that August night, surely they had also come to hear. Her strange opinions had been well advertised.

She started to speak, and her voice and style were cool, rational, an appeal to reason. Her eloquence was of the mind, not of the emotions. She did not whip her audience into hysterical frenzy, like the preachers at the religious revival meeting then taking place in Cincinnati. She had come to town, she said, for the express purpose of doing battle with that revival. She wanted to rally the people of Cincinnati against "the priestcraft," to take up "the cause of insulted reason."

Then Fanny explained her belief in free inquiry—the right to think one's way through any problem without any interference from authority. She left no doubt she was referring to religious authority.

One can only be happy, she continued, if one lives in accordance with a true knowledge of the world. This true knowledge can only come from a person's independent, scientific observations. One must never trust other people's authority, other people's opinions.

Every existing institution—school, government, church, family, marriage—must be tested and examined, not just accepted unquestioningly, tested in the light of true knowledge. This testing will tell us if these institutions are working well or not. If they are not working well, they should be improved or discarded.

Take marriage. (Here the audience must have sucked in its breath and listened in nervous silence.) Marriage made people unhappy. People should love each other freely, without compulsion. Marriage was based on compulsion. It was also based on inequality. Until married women had the same rights as married men—the right to own property, to choose a profession, to make legal contracts, to enjoy an equal education—until then marriage could not be happy, because the husband was the master and the wife was his slave.

But there was hope, said Fanny. America was the one country where all institutions could be examined, evaluated, and if necessary, discarded or changed. America was a free country without a state religion, without a king, without a standing army. The people governed themselves, and they could change things if they wished.

Fanny had great faith in the good sense of the American people. All that was needed was that they be educated and informed. She was sure, for example, that once they saw the "true knowledge" of how evil the slavery of black people was, they would do away with it voluntarily. Clearly, she saw herself as one of the educators of the American people. She would provide them with true knowledge.

She turned to her main enemy, organized religion. She played no favorites. "I am no Christian," she told the crowd, "in the sense usually attached to the word. I am neither Jew nor Gentile, Mohammedan nor Theist. I am but a member of the human family." Asked if there were a God, she would answer, "I don't know."

Above all, she concluded, one must not permit others to think for one. "Receive no man's assertion," she said. "Believe no conviction but your own; and respect not your own until you know that you have examined both sides of every question . . . . Ask *why* of every teacher. Ask *why* of every book."

These were radical ideas. Even more radical was the fact that they were announced in public, calmly, by a young, wealthy, highly educated young woman—a woman who had been born into the British upper class.

Fanny Wright was offering a rich serving of intellectual food to the hungry minds of Cincinnati. In the year 1828—a rebellious, questioning year—Americans were in a mood to listen. Her lecture was an enormous success.

Her English friend Frances Trollope listened. Mrs. Trollope was living in Cincinnati with her children. She had managed to squeeze into the crowded courthouse when she heard that Fanny was coming to town. She was not a woman who was either surprised or impressed very easily. She did not agree at all with her friend's radical ideas. Yet she was astounded at the lecture, and at its impact on the audience.

"In America," she wrote, "where women are guarded by a seven-fold shield of habitual insignificance, it caused an effect that can hardly be described. All my expectation fell far short of the splendor, the brilliance, the overwhelming eloquence of this extraordinary orator."

Hundreds of people came forward to buy subscriptions to Fanny's newspaper, the *New Harmony Gazette.* Delegations from the Ohio River towns of Covington, Hamilton, and Georgetown asked her to come and speak to their people. The leading liberals of Cincinnati cornered her on the platform and urged her to repeat her lecture in the large theater at Main and Sycamore streets.

Only the clergy and the press attacked her. A Catholic priest forbade his parishioners to attend her lectures. Conservatives accused her of "infidelity," the contemporary term for atheism.

She considered these attacks a measure of her success. She described her victory in triumphant words: "A kindling of wrath among the clergy, a reaction in favor of common sense on the part of their followers, an explosion of public sentiment in favor of liberty, liberality, and instructional reform, and a complete exposure of the nothingness of the press . . . ."

Subscriptions to the *New Harmony Gazette* poured in. Letters came from Wheeling, West Virginia, from Baltimore, Philadelphia, and New York, inviting her to speak. Her sister Camilla wrote to friends in Europe: "Her heretical doctrines on religion and morals were received with feelings of the deepest interest and curiosity."

Overnight Fanny Wright had become the voice of

free thought and free inquiry. The dream she had
dreamed had come true. "I have wedded the cause of
human improvement," she had said. And she remembered her girlhood vow . . . .

Chapter 2 BORN RICH

For the poor always ye have with you.
JOHN 12:8

SHE had made that vow when she was a girl in the home of her Aunt Frances Campbell in the little town of Dawlish, in England. But her life had begun sixteen years before that in Dundee, Scotland, in the upside-down year of 1795.

It was twelve years after the Americans had won their freedom from King George III, two years after the French had killed their king, Louis XVI. There were bread riots by the poor in Scotland in 1795. Near London a mob stopped the royal coach and tried to drag the king out. The Irish seamen in the royal navy plotted mutiny. In the Scottish city of Dundee some unknown people erected a forbidden liberty pole.

And on September 6, in Dundee, in the violent year 1795, Frances Wright was born, to join her brother Richard. One and a half years later another girl, Camilla, was born.

A year later both parents died. The children were scattered. Richard went to live with cousins in Glasgow.

Camilla stayed with her nurse in Dundee. Fanny was shipped off to the house of her grandfather, General Duncan Campbell, in London. She was two and a half years old. Everyone said she looked exactly like her father, James.

General Duncan Campbell lived in a rich, warm world, with lots of good food, many horses and carriages, and a small army of servants. Now it was Fanny's world. Servants did everything for her. One washed her face, dressed her, combed her hair, and handed her a handkerchief when she needed one. Another made her bed, brought her food, and picked up everything she dropped almost before it touched the ground. A governess was constantly at her side to instruct her and watch over her playtime.

Because she was a member of a wealthy upper-class family, she was never permitted to do anything for herself. Grandfather Campbell made sure that she was raised like a proper lady—charming, elegant, and helpless.

For Fanny, life in her grandfather's house was like life in prison. When her governess took her for walks, she saw working-class children at play. She envied them. They seemed so happy and free, with nobody standing over them, telling them what to do and what not to do every minute. Once she tried to run after a group of them, but her governess seized her firmly by the arm and scolded her.

"You must not play with those dirty children."

"Why not?"

"Because they are poor," the governess said. "It would never do for a person of good family to be friendly with them."

Fanny asked *Why not?* again—the question was to become her lifelong habit—but the governess merely scowled and dragged her away from the poor children, as if they were infected with some awful disease.

Fanny wished she were poor instead of rich. And then one day she learned exactly what *that* meant. It was shortly after her eighth birthday. She was in the sitting room with Grandfather Campbell when there was a knock at the door. The butler was busy in the kitchen, and with much grumbling, the old general made his way to the front of the house and threw open the door.

A man dressed in filthy rags stood there. He was very thin, and his hair was matted and stringy. He looked extremely weak, as if he could barely stand. His voice was soft and pleading as he asked the general for some food. "I have not eaten in three days," he added.

"Why don't you go to work," the general asked, "instead of begging?"

"I am willing to work, but there are no jobs," the man said. "Give me some food and some clothes, and I will work for you."

"I don't need your help," said the general.

Fanny saw a tear in the man's eye. She felt sorry for him. "If I had some money," she said, "I would give it to you for food."

This seemed to make her grandfather angry. He shut the door on the man. And then he turned to Fanny.

"You are a foolish, simple girl. You know nothing of the world."

One day shortly afterward, she went driving with him in his carriage. The horses were fat and sleek, with big proud heads. Their coats had been combed and curried until they shone in the sunshine. The coachman sat up front in his fine livery, snapping his whip. Behind, a footman stood on the rail of the coach. His job was to jump down, open the door, and help them if they wanted to get out and walk.

As they rode through the streets of London, Fanny saw crowds of people, all of them in rags. They held out their hands as the carriage rolled past, shouting and pleading. Strong-looking young men cried, "A penny for bread, masters!" There were great numbers of hungry women, many of them with three or four little children clinging to their skirts, also crying out for money.

The streets were clotted with people. Those who did not beg were dressed in clothes as ragged and wretched as the others. All of them were pale and thin; some threw angry looks at the fine Campbell coach, the handsome horses, the rich old man and the rich little girl riding inside. They must have looked to Fanny like creatures from another planet.

"Why are there so many poor people in London, Grandfather?" she asked.

"Because they are too lazy to work."

"But rich people do not work, and they are not poor."

"Of course not!" said her grandfather. "It is a shame for a rich man to work."

There was a great curiosity in Fanny that would not let her rest until she had an answer that satisfied her. And she did not have such an answer now. "But why are some people rich while others are poor?"

"Some are born rich, and some are born poor," said the general. "The Bible tells us, *The poor always ye have with you.* God intended it that way."

It occurred to Fanny that if God intended that some should suffer poverty while others enjoyed riches, he must be a very unfair god indeed. But she said nothing about that. Instead she asked, "How did you get rich, Grandfather?"

"I inherited my property from my father, and he from his, and so on down many generations."

"But how did the first rich man get his property?"

The general became impatient. "It is work which produces wealth. If there were no work, there would be no money."

"Well, then," said Fanny thoughtfully, "if it is work which produces wealth, and if rich men do not work, then they must rob the poor to get their riches and that must be the way beggars are made in London."

General Campbell's face grew red. "I do not want to hear any more questions," he said. "You are a bad girl, a spoiled girl. If you go on in this way you will not be able to associate with people of our class. You will be fit

only for that trash in the streets!" And he pointed a
finger in the direction of the crowds of beggars.

Fanny fell silent. She knew she had asked questions
to which her grandfather had no answers.

Had anyone?

Chapter 3 THE MAKING OF A PHILOSOPHER

"Is truth dangerous?"

FRANCES WRIGHT

THE Campbells surrounded her with every luxury. She had servants and tutors, and a fine library of books and maps. She had everything but love. She began to dislike her mother's family, especially Aunt Frances.

Frances Campbell, whose name Fanny bore, had never married. She was tall and pretty and hard. Fanny resolved never to let her become a mother to her.

But Grandfather Campbell had put Fanny in her care, and so Aunt Frances was her legal guardian. She had control of the Wright inheritance, of all of Fanny's money, until she became of age. Under the law Fanny was a ward of chancery—an orphan who would be under the authority of her aunt until the age of twenty-one.

Her body could be controlled, but not her mind. Her thoughts, at least, were free. No one could get inside her. No one could chain up her spirit. She was empress of her own intelligence.

She learned to value intellectual freedom. She discovered that questions could be used as weapons. There were many things adults did not know.

She said to her Sunday School teacher: "You have told me about God's son. But you have never told me about God's wife." The Sunday School teacher told her to be quiet or she would surely go to hell. She knew that meant he did not know how to answer her.

Her mathematics tutor, a brilliant and friendly young man, warned her one day that she was too curious. "Your questions are dangerous," he said.

"Is truth dangerous?" Fanny asked.

"So people say," the tutor replied.

Fanny kept silent. But she thought, *People are afraid of the truth, even if they do not know what it is.*

When Fanny was eleven, her sister, Camilla, came from Scotland to live with them. Aunt Frances, with Grandfather Campbell's permission, took the two girls to live in her house in Dawlish, in the country. Because she was not married, Frances Campbell had considerable freedom. No husband had control over her, only her father, the general.

Now that Camilla was with her, Fanny was happy. Camilla was not rebellious. She did not contradict adults. She tried to please her aunt and her tutors. She was soft and gentle, and she wanted to be friends with everyone. But she was passionately devoted to her sister. When Fanny got into arguments, Camilla always supported her. With Camilla at her side, Fanny had a loyal ally.

Dawlish was a sleepy little Devonshire town. Life crept on—dull, peaceful, respectable. Outwardly Fanny grew into a bored upper-class young woman with a cool manner and a biting tongue. Inwardly she seethed with ideas of revolution. She wanted to overthrow the whole world, beginning with Frances Campbell.

She wrote poetry and then tore it up before anyone could see it. She worried about life, about what it had in store for her. All the while Aunt Frances surrounded the girls with the chains of a conventional upper-class up-bringing, trying to make them into the kind of person the Campbells admired.

One day in June exciting news came from London. Richard was coming for a visit. They had not seen their brother since they had all three been infants in Dundee. Now he was a grown young man of sixteen, a cadet in the service of the great East India Company, on his way to go off to fight in the war against the French. Aunt Frances had promised him five hundred pounds to buy himself a commission, so that he would be an officer. He was coming to get the money, and to thank her for it.

Fanny and Camilla rose at four o'clock on the morning of his arrival and rushed to the window at every sound: a wheel creaking, a step on the stones of the road outside, a noise that might be a horse's hoof striking the cobblestones. When dawn came and the busy day began, they flew down the stairs at every random knock at the door.

It was afternoon before Richard finally arrived in a coach with Grandfather Campbell. The three youngsters looked at each other in a moment of shyness. Then they fell into each other's arms and hugged and kissed and cried tears of happiness. The Wright family was together again.

Richard was tall and handsome. *Father must have looked like that,* Fanny thought. Richard was equally impressed with his sister. "Fanny," he wrote an adult relative, "is as tall as you are, very thin, and extremely pretty."

He stayed with them at Dawlish for the rest of June. The three Wrights went riding together in the country. They spent whole days with each other. Richard did not share his sister Fanny's dislike of the Campbells. But he did not argue with her.

The time came for him to leave for Portsmouth to board ship for India. Before he sailed, he sent her a note with a lock of his hair and some of their mother's. "I believe you have got some of our mother's hair already," he wrote, "but accept this . . . . I am just going on board."

Soon after, the ship was attacked by the French near the island of Madeira. Richard Wright was one of the first to lose his life. At almost the same time Grandfather Campbell died suddenly at his home in London.

Fanny wondered what curse hung over her. She had lost both mother and father while she was still a baby.

Now suddenly both her brother and her grandfather had died. Was this what life was going to be like?

She was only fourteen. The only person left to love was Camilla.

Chapter 4 FANNY WRIGHT DISCOVERS AMERICA

> *"When it shall be said in any country in the world,
> 'My poor are happy; neither ignorance nor distress
> is found among them; my jails are empty of prison-
> ers . . . ,' then may that country boast of its con-
> stitution and its government . . . ."*
>
> THOMAS PAINE

IT wasn't only Fanny's personal life that seemed tragic. Something was wrong with the world.

She read for hours, for days, in her aunt's library. She read the works of Thomas Paine, the English radical who had gone to America and then to France to help the revolutions in both countries. She read Mary Wollstonecraft, who argued for the equality of women.

She had been tutored in French, Italian, Latin, and Greek—like any well-brought-up girl of her class. She read the classical philosophers of Greece and Rome, but she read as well the philosophers of the French Revolution.

Fine books and elaborate libraries were marks of distinction. Aristocratic families collected the great books of the time and displayed them with pride, even if they did not read them very often. The Campbells were proud of their distinguished ancestors, and felt it was their duty to keep and add to the family library.

From this fine library Fanny learned something about the world. She learned that peasants worked like animals on land they did not own. And when they became too sick or too old to work, the landlords turned them out to starve.

Some landlords found grazing sheep and cattle more profitable than raising crops. They drove the peasants off the land to make room for the animals. Others in the north of England and Scotland expelled their peasants and turned their great estates into parks for hunting and fishing.

There was no place for most peasants to go but to the cities. Men and women and children crowded into the slums of London and Liverpool. But there was not enough work in the cities. Many of the poor became beggars. Others turned to stealing.

The landowners were not wicked people. Fanny's relatives—all the Campbells—were landowners. All their friends in Dawlish and London came from well-to-do families.

These families had fine manners. They lived in handsome houses, with carpets from Persia, glass from Italy, furniture from France. Their silver and china were exquisite. They had large libraries filled with interesting books. Many of the women were people of taste and culture. But their class benefitted from the misery and hunger of the poor.

Fanny read for hours in the library of the Campbell house in Dawlish. She read newspapers and journals. She learned more and more about the world. She learned that there were poor and rich in all countries, not just in England. The whole world was like that.

The books described but did not explain the world. They did not explain the bloody slaughter of the wars with Napoleon. These wars had been going on almost since Fanny's birth, and now, when she was sixteen, armies still marched back and forth across Europe. Ships at sea attacked each other and sent whole boatloads of men to death by drowning. Great cities were burned to the ground. Millions of innocent people were tortured, starved, and murdered.

In all her life there had not been one year of peace. The world seemed insane. Adults were unable to explain it. War and hunger seemed as natural to them as the sun and the wind.

She did not think they were natural. She felt there must be a reason for human misery. Questions grew in her mind:

Why must the rich live off the poor?
Why could not all people have enough to eat?
Why was the world such a violent, troubled place?
Why did there have to be war?

Mary Wollstonecraft's book *A Vindication of the*

Rights of Woman struck a spark in her heart. Why were
women treated as inferior creatures? Even rich women
like herself, even Aunt Frances, could not own property
and had no legal rights, once they married. The law put
wives under the absolute authority of their husbands.

If Aunt Frances married, all her property—and all of
Fanny's property—would pass into the hands of her
husband. Aunt Frances would still be Fanny's guardian, but Aunt Frances would now have a legal guardian
over her—her husband. The law made men rulers over
their wives and children.

Once a rich woman married, she lost her wealth and
freedom. In fact, she lost more by marriage than a poor
woman who owned no property. Some upper-class
women therefore put off marriage for as long as they
could.

Was that why Aunt Frances had never married?

"A woman ought not to give up a single natural right
to a man by marriage," she thought, "not even her
body. *She* should decide how many children there
should be. And they should bear *her* name instead of
their father's."

She sat for hours, reading and thinking. There was,
she decided, an evil secret that lay behind the madness
of the world. If one could learn that secret, perhaps one
could solve the problem of human misery.

She stood one day before the pier glass, a tall slender
girl with thick chestnut curls atop her large handsome
face. She looked at herself out of her deep blue eyes and
swore her solemn vow: she would devote her life to

searching out the secret that lay behind the world's misery. She would make the world a better place. Instead of living a rich and idle life, she would spend her wealth and energies to help others.

A few days later she sat rummaging through a chest of old books that lay half hidden in a corner of her aunt's library. She found a book by the Italian historian Carlo Botta. The book's title was *History of the War for Independence of the United States of America.*

She was curious. She had never heard of the United States of America. None of the books in Aunt Frances' library had mentioned such a country. Nor had she read about it in the newspapers. She picked the book up and began to read, slowly, translating as she read. When she finished the book, she felt strange. It seemed as if one part of the world was different. She had discovered something new.

"Life was full of promise," she remembered feeling years later. "There existed a country consecrated to freedom."

She closed the book with a secret promise to herself. She would go and see that strange and hopeful country as soon as she could. She would tell her ambition to no one, not even Camilla.

But why had she never heard of such a place? Was the book fiction? Perhaps there *was* no United States of America!

She raced through her aunt's library, plunging from shelf to shelf. There were no other books that mentioned such a country. She turned to the atlases. The first she opened did not show the United States. On the North American continent only British colonies were drawn. She did not realize that the map had been made and the book published before 1776, nor did she realize that none of the books in the library were new enough to mention the young nation.

She hunted eagerly for information about the United States. The papers reported the war news from Europe, but they printed not a word about Britain's former colonies.

No one ever talked about America.

Finally she discovered a newer map with the words "United States of America" printed along the Atlantic Coast. There *was* such a place. She had not been reading fiction.

What if Botta had exaggerated? Was it really the kind of country his book said it was?

She began to read modern British histories. She read Belsham's *History of George III* in a friend's library. It described the thirteen former colonies and their new government. There was a United States of America, and it did not have a king. It was not governed by a hereditary aristocracy; titles such as count and duke and baron were against the law.

The government was said to be in the hands of the common people. Even the first words of its Constitution began, "We, the people of the United States . . . ." It did not have an official state religion. There really were men named Thomas Jefferson, John Adams, and James Madison.

And then suddenly a year later *everyone* was talking about America.

She was visiting a retired admiral she knew, a blind old man full of military passion. That day he was also full of angry curses.

"What is the matter, sir?" He reminded her of Grandfather Campbell.

"You are my good angel, Fanny," he sighed. "Come to pour oil on my troubled waters."

"But what is troubling you so?"

"It is those wicked rebels again. There is nothing you can do."

"What rebels?"

"Those impudent rebels in our former American colonies. It's an old story—the less said the better. They are picking up our ships again, all over the ocean."

Fanny fell quiet. But her heart sang silently. Her gallant little promised land was tormenting the powerful British Empire!

From that day she cared nothing for England's battles with Napoleon. She devoted all her attention to the crumbs of news about America's War of 1812. Whenever she heard that the Americans had sent one of his majesty's ships to the bottom of the sea, she cheered and applauded.

But she cheered and applauded silently. She did not dare to voice her sentiments, not even to Camilla. She did not wish to be arrested as a traitor to the crown.

Chapter 5 GLASGOW

*"I think I have done with churches.
When I can hear of one that does
honor to God and good to man it
shall have my presence and my love."*
FRANCES WRIGHT

WHEN she was eighteen, Fanny told Aunt Frances and
the rest of the Campbells she no longer wanted to live
with them.

She was still legally under age and without any con-
trol over the considerable property her father had left.
But she insisted on moving out, nevertheless, and with
Camilla's support she made it stick. The two girls left
Dawlish and went to live with their father's uncle in
Scotland. Fanny had nothing further to do with Aunt
Frances.

Great-uncle James Mylne was professor of moral philosophy at Glasgow University. His home was small
and dark and crowded. Fanny and Camilla, who had
had their own separate rooms in Dawlish, now had to
share a narrow bedchamber. The Mylnes were poor
compared with the Campbells. There was nothing lovely

or gracious about their home, no fine silver and table linen, no exquisite carpets or imported furniture.

Glasgow seemed different, too. It was a busy, dirty, noisy city. Its buildings of great dank stone almost hid the weak yellow sun. There were miserable slums nearby. Just a few squares away from the Mylne home, over the black cobblestones, the ancient walls of Glasgow University rose high above the street. It had been built in the year 1450.

The city was filled with merchants and businessmen whose politics were very different from those of the Campbells and their land-owning friends. The Scottish middle class were Whigs, not Tories. They hated the king and wanted Parliament to rule the country.

They sympathized with the United States. Some of them sympathized with the French. Many had read Thomas Paine. Those who were Presbyterians despised the official Church of England.

The middle-class leaders of Glasgow lived a different life from anything Fanny and Camilla had seen in England. They looked up to education and science. They looked down on idleness, luxury, and wasteful living. They despised hunting and war.

They judged a man by his personal success, instead of by his family heritage or the size of his estates. They thought more of a man who had been born poor and had made himself rich than of a man who had been born to privilege because his father was a lord.

Fanny loved Glasgow. Despite the noise, the dirt, the

crowding, and the discomfort, she felt like a bird let out of its cage. Glasgow was freedom.

She learned about the father she had never known. She learned that he had been highly educated and had traveled all across Europe. He had been a member of scientific societies. He had known and talked with Adam Smith, the famous political economist. He had been an outspoken liberal.

She heard from old friends the story of his secret support of Thomas Paine. She heard of his risking his liberty and his life to collect money for a cheap edition of Paine's great revolutionary book, *The Rights of Man.* She rushed to read the book again as soon as she heard the news.

She discovered an exciting family legend. Her father had to row out into the harbor of the River Tay one dark night to dump papers into the water—papers that linked him to the illegal publication of Paine's book and to a radical organization, the Society of the Friends of the People. Two of his friends had been caught at meetings of the society. They had been arrested, tried, convicted, and transported to Australia.

She thrilled to discover that she and her father had the same radical opinions. How remarkable that this should be so, considering that she had been raised in England without any contact with her Scottish relatives!

She drew support from his writings. They showed, she said, "a somewhat singular coincidence in views between a father and daughter separated by death." One

statement she found in his personal papers sounded a
special echo in her soul. "The spirit of law," James
Wright had written, "and the conduct of government
ought constantly to change according to existing circumstances and the temper of the age."

Change was becoming her watchword.

She was stimulated by the lively political discussions
in the Mylne household. Uncle James and his friends
were not afraid of intellectual challenge and debate.
They loved to argue about politics and philosophy.

Compared with the frivolous and boring conversa-
tions at the Campbells' dinner table, the talk at the
Mylnes' was intoxicating. The Campbells had talked
about hunting, shooting, and drinking. Sometimes the
men talked about women while the women gossiped.
When the men talked about women, they sounded to
Fanny as if they were talking about an inferior class of
human beings.

The Mylnes talked about the rights of men and
women, about war and peace and science. They talked
about France and America.

When Fanny requested library privileges at Glasgow
University, the librarian, Professor Muirhead, took her
to a small room in a distant corner of the old stone
building. It was filled from floor to ceiling with books,
pamphlets, and documents. "Here," said the professor,
"is everything about the American colonies that has
ever appeared in print. It is here for you to take and use
as you wish."

For two years Fanny buried herself in her studies of America. "Here," she wrote later, "I found the colonial history of the United States, the struggle of the seven years' war for independence, and a free government, a President elected by the people, no nobility, no state church or tax to support the clergy.

"After reading Jefferson's Declaration of Independence, the most masterly piece ever penned by man, I resolved that the United States was the place to put into practice my long cherished notions of reform. I made up my mind to visit that country."

She buried herself in philosophy, too. She found herself drawn to the teachings of the ancient Greek scholar Epicurus. Epicurus taught that man should heed only the evidence of his five senses. Knowledge, he said, came from seeing, hearing, touching, tasting, and smelling. Epicurus distrusted knowledge that came from speculation or logic. He especially distrusted knowledge that was handed down by superior authority.

Epicurus' ideas fitted Fanny's developing philosophy. She had lost her faith in religious leaders who claimed to know God's wishes and wanted their followers to take their word for it. She had concluded that she should trust her own ideas more than the opinions of others. The so-called experts of the adult world— priests, ministers, teachers, writers—seemed to be ignorant and dishonest.

They were wrong about the world, and they lied to cover up their lack of knowledge. They could not an-

swer her questions about war, poverty, and injustice.
They could explain nothing. She decided she would
have to become her own expert.
  Why should not every man and woman become his or
her own expert? Could they not see and read and hear
for themselves? Why should they swallow the stale and
false opinions of others?
  One could be sure of nothing one could not prove
scientifically, that is, by observation. Since one could
not observe God, one could not say that God existed.
On the other hand, one could not say that God did *not*
exist. Fanny would have said: there is no evidence either way, and so one cannot claim that either statement
is false or that either statement is true.
  Thus she developed her own modern version of Epicureanism. She wrote a book about it, in the style of
Plato's dialogues. But she was not bold enough to put
her name to it and have it published. She was still only a
very young woman, barely twenty. Mary Wollstonecraft
had been thirty-three when *A Vindication of the Rights of
Woman* had been published. And *that* had caused a
scandal.
  One day Fanny passed the harbor, and saw a ship
loaded with emigrants about to sail across the Atlantic.
They were desperately poor Scottish peasants, driven
from their Highland farms by landlords who had no
more need for their labor. Some of the peasants had
sold themselves as indentured servants, some as white
slaves, to pay their passage to the new world.
  Fanny observed one old grandmother with seven

grandchildren in her charge. "These seemingly helpless people were bound not for Canada," she noted, "but the States."

In a year she would be twenty-one and her own mistress. The Wright money would be hers. She would not have to ask Aunt Frances' permission for anything.

She would follow the emigrants to America.

II
Promised Land

MIRANDA. *O brave new world that hath such people in it!*

PROSPERO. *'Tis new to thee.*
—SHAKESPEARE, *The Tempest*

Chapter 6 BRAVE NEW WORLD

"Everything in the neighborhood of this city exhibits the appearance of life and cheerfulness. The purity of the air, the brilliancy of the unspotted heavens . . . there is something in all this . . . which exhilarates the spirits . . . . It was for the first time in my life that I had drawn a clear breath."

FRANCES WRIGHT, ON FIRST
SEEING NEW YORK CITY

THREE years after she had watched the poor Scottish peasants sail for America she fulfilled her silent promise to follow them.

But only on the day they walked up the gangplank of the packet ship *Amity* in Liverpool did Fanny reveal their secret to Uncle James—she and Camilla were going to America. It was August 2, 1818. Until that moment, their destination had been kept from everyone but Mrs. Rabina Craig Millar.

Rabina Millar was Uncle James's sister-in-law. She was a widow; her husband had been an especially good friend of Fanny's father. Both men had held the same political opinions; they were radicals, in sympathy with the French Revolution. The Millars had had to run away to America the year before Fanny was born to avoid arrest by the police.

They had lived in exile in Philadelphia and New York. There they had met other British, Irish, and Scottish exiles. The administration of President George Washington had welcomed them and offered them a safe refuge from British repression. After her husband died and the repression ended, Rabina Millar had returned to England.

The older woman had become something of a mother to Fanny. She encouraged her, loved her, and petted her. Her tales of life in America excited Fanny. When she learned of Fanny's plans she gave her letters of introduction to old friends still in the United States.

Now, at the last minute, Uncle James came to the dock with Rabina Millar to see the girls off on the *Amity*. When he found out where they were going, he tried to talk them out of the trip. In those days the proper voyage for a young lady of classical education was a tour of Greece and Italy. Uncle James shrewdly pointed out that Fanny's studies in Epicurus' philosophy would make such a trip more meaningful to her.

But Fanny thought that a nation of free men was much more interesting than a country of oppressed people. Italy was then under the rule of Austria; Greece under the rule of Turkey. "The sight of Italy," she told her uncle, "would break my heart."

Uncle James listened good-humoredly and remarked that she was very much "the child of her father and must have inherited her views and principles."

Uncle James preferred Camilla to Fanny. Camilla was soft and gentle and very much what a young lady was expected to be. Fanny was too assertive, too aggressive, too fond of giving her own opinions. He thought this made her character somewhat masculine.

None of this was a secret to Fanny. She knew that men found it hard to accept a woman who had a mind of her own. She knew, too, that their admiration for softness and gentleness in women masked a form of contempt for what they considered to be weakness.

Fanny agreed with Mary Wollstonecraft. "Would men but generously snap our chains," the women's champion had written, "and be content with rational fellowship instead of slavish obedience, they would find us more observant daughters, more affectionate sisters, more faithful wives, more reasonable mothers—in a word, better citizens. We should then love them with true affection, because we would learn to respect ourselves."

On Thursday evening, September 2, 1818, just as the sun was about to set, the *Amity* sailed up New York harbor to its pier in the East River. She carried a cargo of dry goods and hardware from Liverpool, and she brought the latest news.

The news from England was that the spinners in Manchester were still on strike. "Still without work," re-

ported the New York newspapers the next day. "Male
and female, they continue to parade the streets crying
out for higher wages."

The *Amity* also carried passengers, sixteen of them.
The list included two young women traveling alone,
said the papers: "Miss F. Wright and Miss C. Wright."

The girls came down the gangplank with their belong-
ings and looked around for a carriage in the twilight. It
was very hot, but everyone was friendly and polite. Men
bustled about loading wagons and taking charge of
freight and luggage.

Something is missing here, Fanny said to Camilla.
There are no beggars. No swarms of hungry people
crying out for pennies for food.

The workingmen wore good heavy jackets. Their
white shirts were open at the neck. They had on light
straw hats with big sun-shading brims. Their faces were
sunburned. They acted friendly, and yet proud and independent.

Riding through the streets to their boardinghouse, the
Wright girls found New York a pretty city. The streets
were wide and clean, the houses neatly painted, with tall
poplar trees rising behind them.

The streets, Fanny noticed, were "democratic." They
had a raised curb to protect ordinary walkers from
being run down by the carriages of the wealthy people.
In Paris and London the narrow streets offered no such
protection to the walker. The coaches of aristocrats
came thundering through, forcing walkers to run into

the doorways of houses for fear of being killed or crippled.

There wasn't much to look at in the way of architecture—nothing ornamental or artistic or grand in the city's public buildings. But on the other hand there were no slums. "No dark alleys," Fanny noted. "No hovels . . . no dank and gloomy cellars."

At the boardinghouse they had some fruit and tea, and sat and chatted with the landlady. It was a very still, hot night. All the windows and doors were open. While they talked, a strange sound filled the air. They had heard it beneath the din and bustle of the harbor while the *Amity* was unloading. But now in the quiet the sound was so loud they could hardly ignore it. It was a sound they had never heard before, a sort of tic-a-tac, a humming or buzzing or chirping, as if something was being rubbed rhythmically against something else.

The landlady chatted on as if she heard nothing. Finally Fanny could stand it no longer. "I suppose those must be frogs," she said suddenly.

"Frogs? Where?"

"I don't know where," Fanny said. "But somewhere certainly."

"Not here," said the landlady.

"Then what is that noise?"

"I don't hear any noise."

Fanny insisted. The landlady listened carefully. Finally she said, "I don't hear anything at all except the katydids."

"Katydids? Who are they?"

At this the lady laughed. "Not who but what," she said. "They are insects—something like grasshoppers. Don't you have them in England?"

As a matter of fact, they did not. There were no katydids in England, or, for that matter, anywhere else in the world. Later Fanny would have a chance to hold one of them in her hand and to marvel at how much larger it was than the ordinary European grasshopper, and how brilliant a green.

The existence of katydids was another difference between America and Europe.

Chapter 7 "AUTHOR! AUTHOR!"

"Here is the country where Truth may lift her voice without fear. Where the words of Freedom may not only be read in the closet, but heard from the stage."

FRANCES WRIGHT

THE New York City the Wright girls came to in 1818 was a city just recovering from the hard times of the War of 1812. That war had ended three years earlier. Business was finally picking up.

New York had suffered bitterly during the war. It was a city that lived by trade. During the war, the navies of France and England had made it impossible for ships to come into or go out of the port. President Jefferson's earlier embargo and then the wartime blockade had been as tight as a kite string. The end of the war meant jobs and prosperity.

A tenth of the hundred thousand New Yorkers were black. Most of them were free people. They were laborers, sailors, longshoremen, coachmen, servants, cooks, barbers, and hairdressers. Many were unemployed. They tried to keep alive by collecting junk and rags and selling them. They were unemployed because white people would not permit free blacks to work beside them.

In another nine years the few slaves in New York would be free. The state had passed an emancipation act in 1799. On July 4, 1827, slavery would be illegal in New York State.

Prices, Fanny wrote back to Rabina Millar, were extraordinarily high. In the Washington Market prime beef was $.12½ a pound, and a chicken cost $.28. Turkeys, those strange birds found only in America, were $1.56 apiece. Some said the prices were so high because of the extremely bitter winters of the past two years, which had killed many animals.

The entire nation was going through a period of harmony and contentment now that the war had ended. The Federalist party, which had opposed the war and been strong in New York and New England, had disappeared. The great majority of those Americans who voted supported the Democratic-Republican party of Thomas Jefferson, James Madison, and President James Monroe.

Politicians and historians have called the period from 1815 to 1823 the Era of Good Feeling. It was a time when the American experiment seemed to be succeeding. If one ignored the 1,500,000 slaves and the 250,000 badly treated free blacks—and most white people did ignore them—it looked as if heaven on earth might arise in the young republic. Few people who thought about it at all foresaw any problems clouding the future of the United States of America.

Fanny saw none. She was affected by the public atmosphere. Happiness was what she had hoped to find. She was not looking for problems; she was looking for confirmation of her own opinions. She saw only what she wanted to see: the virtues of the first country where common people seemed to rule the nation.

New York City was not only a bustling commercial metropolis. It was also becoming a center of culture to rival the New England metropolis, Boston, and the Quaker city, Philadelphia. It had built libraries and museums. The New-York Historical Society had been founded just fourteen years earlier.

There were two theaters in New York, the Circus and the Park. The Circus was offering a horse show. At the Park there was a double bill: *Pizarro,* a tragedy of the Spanish conquest of Peru, and *Poor Soldier,* a musical farce.

Fanny was more than a bit interested in the theater. In her luggage was a number of plays she had written during her years of study in Scotland. One of these plays was a drama about democracy, called *Altorf.* It concerned the revolutionary struggle of the Swiss against their Austrian rulers, and had been inspired by the story of William Tell, which it very much resembled.

In the back of her mind Fanny fancied herself a great writer. It may have been her wish to become a famous dramatist on the strength of *Altorf.* If that was the case, she was bold beyond belief. The theater was considered, in those days, a place of degeneracy and vice. Well-bred people did not write plays or appear in them on the stage. No well-brought-up young woman had anything to do with actors or actresses. The American theater suffered from an inferiority complex. All the actors were English. The producers were English. If a play was successful in London or if an actor had achieved fame there, then there was some chance of success in New York, Boston, or Philadelphia. Despite their patriotic hatred of everything British, many Americans were anxious to copy the mother country's ways.

None of these facts discouraged Fanny. She had tried to get the play produced in England. She had sent a copy to the famous actor John Kemble. She had sent it under a man's name because she knew no one would look at a play written by a woman.

But apparently even a false name did not help. Kemble returned the play unopened and unread. Then she went to a young cousin her own age, James Watson. Watson was in love with Fanny. He would do anything for her. But this he could not do. He was unable to get *Altorf* read by any theater manager in London.

Now, in New York, romance again came to Fanny's aid. This time she was successful.

She met young William Theobald Wolfe Tone, the only son of the Irish patriot of the same name. Wolfe Tone the elder had led the uprising of the United Irishmen against the British crown in 1798. He had been caught, tried, and condemned to death as a traitor. His widow and young son had fled to the United States, the only country in which the family of a revolutionary or a political radical could feel safe.

Young Wolfe Tone fell in love with tall, beautiful Fanny. For her part she thought him an interesting and exciting young man. She liked him as much for his father's revolutionary past as for his own personal charm, which was considerable.

Tone was very popular in New York. As the son of the famous patriot he found all doors open to him. The large colony of Irish exiles, headed by Dr. William McNevin, an old friend of Rabina Millar's, had taken him in as one of their own.

Among the Irish exiles the memory of Thomas Paine was also popular. Many of them had known him personally. Fanny and Camilla quickly found these radical social circles. One night Fanny read her play to a small group which included Wolfe Tone. He listened carefully and made many useful comments. Everyone thought the play an exciting romance. The fact that it was written in Shakespearean blank verse made it especially attractive and fashionable.

Wolfe Tone could move in theatrical circles where a well-bred unmarried young woman was barred. He wrote a prologue to *Altorf* and took it, under his own name, to the manager of the Park Theater. He was able to persuade him to produce the play.

There was plenty of excited publicity about *Altorf* during rehearsals. A few people thought it was written by Wolfe Tone himself, a rumor which stirred up public interest. As opening night approached, the papers published advance reports concerning the play.

The New York *Columbian,* one of the city's more ardent republican papers, compared the writing to that of Byron and Scott and boasted that the author "has trusted his work . . . a tale of freedom, to the feelings of the only nation where the cause of freedom dare to be asserted."

The *Columbian* was sure that the author was American and a man. It insisted that there was no dramatic writer in all England who could write as good a play. It closed its literary comments on a political note: "We wish success to this play on another ground—it is a republican play, and we are really tired with always weeping at the sorrows of kings or queens, lords or ladies, as if our sympathy would be degraded if it ever descended below the peerage."

Altorf opened on a snowy night in February. The theater was filled to capacity, and not only with regular playgoers who had come to see their favorite actor, the Englishman James Wallack, in a new and unknown role. There was a turnout of the city's Irish colony, drawn by the name of Wolfe Tone. There were also a few patriots who came to see what they believed to be a native American play.

A few distinguished citizens came, too. Fanny had often been entertained at the home of Charles Wilkes, an old friend of Rabina Millar's and the Wright girls' financial adviser and guardian in the United States.

Many of Wilkes's friends had met and listened to her, and knew she had a strong interest in the play.

Fanny and Camilla sat in a box with Wolfe Tone.

Altorf was a success. The New York *Evening Post* described what it called the greatest round of applause in the history of the Park Theater. "At every fall of the curtain between the acts peals of approbation resounded throughout the house, and at the end of the play loud cries of bravo! author! *Altorf*! from box, pit, and gallery." The applause was so loud at the end that the *Post*'s drama critic could not hear the actress who delivered the epilogue.

It was Fanny's first triumph. She went home through the snowy streets on clouds of happiness. She was sure her career as a writer had begun. That night she sent off a long chatty letter to Rabina Millar.

She described the cries of "Author! Author!" and her mixture of happiness and frustration. She knew the cries were for Wolfe Tone, and in fact many of the Irish in the audience as they applauded had looked knowingly at their box.

But luck was against Fanny. The next day, February 20, the papers reported that General Andrew Jackson, hero of the battle of New Orleans and of the war against the Seminole Indians, was to visit the city. He was coming to New York to celebrate Washington's Birthday, and in all the wild excitement the city completely forgot everything else, including the new play at the Park Theater.

Great plans were made for the two-day visit. Banquets, parades, and testimonials were organized. A grand ball by the Fourteenth Regiment was planned for the City Hotel, the biggest public house in the city. Governor DeWitt Clinton was coming to town to lead the celebration.

At the Park Theater *Altorf* was taken off and *Pizarro* was put back on. Jackson's role as a killer of Seminole Indians and an invader of Spanish Florida was just then being debated in Congress. *Pizarro,* a play about the Spanish conquest and murder of the Incas, was felt to be more suitable entertainment for Jackson than a play about Swiss freedom.

Altorf was given two more performances after the celebrations were over. But despite its popularity among patriotic Americans, it was a financial failure, and it lost money. Still, Fanny was encouraged. She sent it off to a publisher in Philadelphia under her own name.

She added a preface addressed to the American people. She thanked them for the way the play had been received. "Whatever may be its success hereafter," she wrote, "I shall never forget that as the work of a nameless author it was accepted by the Theatre of New York and received with applause by an American audience."

Then she took a slap at the English theater. "England pretends to an unshackled press, but there is not a stage in England from which the dramatist might breathe the sentiments of enlightened patriotism and republican liberty. In America alone might such a stage be formed."

Wolfe Tone left New York shortly after that to enlist

in the United States Army. He could find no career for himself except as a professional soldier. And he had discovered that while Fanny liked him well enough she had no intention of marrying him. Perhaps she did not love him as much as he loved her. They never met again.

Fanny sent copies of *Altorf* to a number of important people. One was Thomas Jefferson, living in retirement on his estate at Monticello. Jefferson wrote back, thanking her for the book and telling her he had read it "with great pleasure and sees in it that excellent moral which gives dignity and usefulness to poetry."

She in turn thanked him and told him how proud she was of his approval. "Mingled with the affection I feel for the young and free America," she added, "is the reverence I feel for the name of Mr. Jefferson."

Altorf made money as a book, enough money to make it easier for the Wright sisters to continue their original plan of a journey through "young and free America."

Chapter 8 TRUE BELIEVER

> *"I may have been sometimes hasty, and therefore, mistaken in my judgments . . . . It is possible that a citizen of America may detect slight errors . . . ."*
> FRANCES WRIGHT

FANNY was a true believer in American democracy long before she set foot on the *Amity*. Much of what she believed about the United States was true; much proved to be false. She saw the country through the eyes of an ardent twenty-four-year-old radical. She was disgusted with reactionary Europe and anxious to find everything perfect in the great experiment across the ocean.

Other European travelers came to America with opposite prejudices. They viewed Americans as lower-class colonists who had revolted against their "betters." They came to sneer. Fanny came to praise and flatter. She had no trouble doing so. The unpleasant truths about the new republic she ignored, excused, or explained.

The two Wright sisters set out in the hot summer of

1819 to tour the northern and eastern states. They were to travel from New York up to the Canadian border and as far west as Niagara Falls and Lake Erie, and then go south to Washington, D.C. There they would observe the national capital and the government in action.

Farther south Fanny would not go. She was well aware that the slavery of black people was the most serious shortcoming of the United States. It was a violation of the noble words in the Declaration of Independence. It was clear to the world that when the Americans spoke of "We, the people," in the Preamble to the Constitution, they meant only "We, the *white* people."

"As regards the southern states," she wrote to Rabina Millar, "I have ever felt a secret reluctance to visit their territory. The sight of slavery is revolting everywhere, but to inhale the impure breath of its pestilence in the free winds of America is odious beyond all that imagination can conceive."

It was typical of Fanny to avoid whatever was unpleasant. She had refused to visit Italy because she could not bear the sight of the Italians oppressed by the Austrians. She would not visit the South because she did not want to face the horror of slavery.

She wrote long letters to Mrs. Millar. Many of these were published two years later in a book about America. They became an important source of information for Europeans interested in what might be going on in the former British colonies.

The sisters were in high spirits. It was no easy matter

for two unmarried young women to travel through the countryside outside the big cities. Roads were difficult and dangerous, coach travel uncomfortable and tiring. The country inns and taverns along the way had rough accommodations of a sort that privileged young Englishwomen would not find easy to bear.

But Fanny was brave. When she was in pursuit of an idea nothing could stop her. Just as she could ignore the unpleasantness of slavery, she could ignore personal hardship and discomfort. She was filled with enthusiasm, determined to find everything as good as it could be in this best of all possible new worlds. Loyal Camilla saw everything through the eyes of sisterly devotion.

Fanny's enthusiasm apparently aroused enthusiasm in return in all who met her. Perhaps the glowing picture she painted was the reflection of the warm and friendly reception she received. Everything seemed perfect, even the manners of the people she met. "I verily believe," she said, "that you might travel from the Canada frontier to the Gulf of Mexico, or from the Atlantic to the Missouri, and never receive from a *native-born citizen* a rude word, it being understood always that you never *give one.*"

Dear to her heart was the status of women. Wherever she went, she was a shrewd observer of how her sex was treated. "The condition of women," she wrote, "affords in all countries the best criterion by which to judge the character of the men."

By this test the character of American men rated high. She was impressed with women's educational opportunities, especially in New England. "In some states," she said, "colleges for girls are established." By "colleges," she probably meant academies—similar to today's high schools. Secondary education for women was still a new idea in 1819.

She discovered that ideas about what was a proper education for a girl were quite different from those of Europe. "The prejudices still to be found in Europe, though now indeed somewhat antiquated, which would confine the female library to romances, poetry and belles-lettres, and female conversation to the last new publication, bonnet, and [dance step] are entirely unknown here. The women are assuming their place as thinking beings . . . ."

The treatment of women by men enchanted her. American men were tender, gallant, and considerate. "In travelling," Fanny wrote, "I have myself often met with refinement of civility from men, whose exterior promised only the roughness of the mechanic or working farmer, that I should only have looked for from the polished gentleman."

Had she traveled south, she would have seen black women forced to do field labor. Just as American rights did not extend to black people, American courtesy and good manners did not include black women. In this respect Fanny was as blind as other white observers. Blacks just did not seem to exist.

"No field labor," she wrote, "is ever imposed upon a woman, and I believe that it would outrage the feelings of an American whatever be his station, should he see her engaged in any toil seemingly unsuited to her strength."

Young, unmarried, inexperienced, Fanny was so overcome with delight at what she observed about the treatment of women that she came to the conclusion that American marriages must be perfect. "The sober happiness of married life is here found in perfection."

Fanny and Camilla went up the Hudson River, visited West Point, stopped briefly at Albany ("the town is old and shabby," thought Fanny), and there set out westward through the Mohawk Valley. They wanted to visit the towns and settlements of the New York frontier.

Wherever they went, they mingled with the people and took careful notes. In their pretty dresses, with their gracious manners, they must have been a charming sight to the rugged western farmers and backwoodsmen.

Of greatest charm was their cheery outlook. Their spirits remained high. "What is there in life more pleasing," Fanny wrote at the start of this most hazardous part of their journey, "than to set forward on a journey with a light heart, a fine sun in the heavens above you, and the earth breathing freshness and fragrance after a summer rain?"

The sisters traveled the way ordinary Americans did. "If our journey was rough," she wrote Rabina Millar, "it was at least very cheerful, the weather beautiful, and our companions good-humored, intelligent, and accommodating. I know not whether to recommend the stagecoach or wagon (for you are sometimes put into the one and sometimes into the other) as the best mode of travelling. This must depend on the temper of the traveller. "If he wants to see people as well as things—to hear intelligent remarks upon the country and its inhabitants . . . if he be of an easy temper, not incommoded with trifles . . . and if too he can bear a few jolts (*not* a few) and can suffer to be driven sometimes too quickly over a rough road and sometimes too slowly over a smooth one—then let him by all means fill a corner in the [stagecoach]."

She compared life in America with life in England: "I cannot help contrasting the condition of the American with that of the English farmer: no tithes, no grinding taxes, no bribes received or offered by electioneering candidates or their agents, no anxious fears as to the destiny of his children and their future . . . ."

With Americans of the West she expressed a racist fear of the Indians, the first inhabitants and rightful owners of the land. Like the backwoodsmen she met, she was afraid that they would someday drive the white invaders away and reclaim their property. Indians, she decided, were dangerous and inferior.

"The savage, with all his virtues," she said, "and he has some virtues, is still savage." With the bloody wars of Napoleonic Europe fresh in her memory she was still so blinded by racial bigotry as to add: "The increase and spread of the white population at the expense of the red is, as it were, the triumph of peace over violence."

One of her earliest and strongest beliefs was that the mind must be free from rules and restrictions. She con-

sidered the church the greatest and most oppressive of
all restrictions placed upon human intelligence. This
was especially true in Europe, where the government
and established religion were allied. People in Europe
were forced to support the church of the ruling monarch
despite their own feelings. In all European countries not
changed by the French Revolution, education and even
scientific writings were in the hands of the religious establishment.

On the subject of religion she was a clear-thinking
and careful observer. Because she took it so seriously,
she did not fall into the traps of false optimism and ex-
cessive enthusiasm.

"Travellers contradict each other," she noted
shrewdly. "Some write the Americans have no religion,
and others that they are a race of fanatics."

She found them to be neither. Some Americans were
very religious. Some were not. "There are sections of the
country where some might think thre is too much [reli-
gion]. This has long been said of New England."

In Connecticut, the year before, the state had stopped
supporting the Congregational church. But in neighbor-
ing Massachusetts official support and public tax funds
were still given to the Congregationalists.

There were other contradictions in New England, despite its rigid Puritan tradition. "There was," she found,
"a considerable body scattered throughout the community who are attached to no establishment, but as they
never trouble their neighbors with their opinions, neither do their neighbors trouble them with theirs."

Because religion was not forced on people by the government, she concluded, "every man enjoys his own opinion without any arguing over the matter." This was important. To Fanny it was the single most significant aspect of American life.

After an exciting visit to the falls of the Genesee River (where Camilla almost fell into the water) and to Niagara Falls, the girls spent a short time in Canada. Fanny noted what she called the unhappiness of the Canadians and attributed it to the fact that they were not independent but were still a colony of England.

In the fall of 1819, with the weather turning cold and Fanny suffering from a slight fever (she was the weaker sister physically, but she drove herself harder), the girls turned south. New York was in the midst of a yellow-fever epidemic, so they bypassed the city and spent the winter in New Brunswick, New Jersey.

There the Wright girls met the John Garnett family and their four daughters—Harriet, Julia, Maria, and Fanny. The Garnetts had come over from England in 1797 because John Garnett was a radical thinker in sympathy with the ideas of the French and American revolutions. The Wright and Garnett girls became close friends, especially Fanny and Harriet.

In nearby Philadelphia, Fanny saw *Altorf* produced one more time. This time she had not needed Wolfe Tone or any other go-between. She herself had persuaded the manager of the Arch Theater to put it on. It was welcomed just as strongly by the press as it had been when it opened in New York back in February. She found Philadelphia delightful. "I never walked the streets of any city with so much satisfaction . . . . I am not sure that the streets have not too many angles and straight lines to be pleasing to the eye, but they have so much the air of cheerfulness, cleanliness, and comfort that it would be quite absurd to find fault with them. The side pavements are regularly washed every morning . . . ."

In April 1820, Fanny and Camilla went to Washington. They missed the congressional debate on the Missouri Compromise, but they did hear Henry Clay, the great Kentucky orator.

The Missouri Compromise was an attempt to decide which of the western territories would enter the Union as free states and which as slave. On the subject of slavery Fanny was inaccurate, evasive, and naïve.

She described it as a temporary evil. She described the black slaves—of whom apparently she had not seen a single one—as childlike individuals who ought not to be freed until they were "ready" for freedom. She did not say when that would be.

She apologized and made excuses for slavery. This reflected the opinions of those Americans she most admired. Thomas Jefferson owned slaves. He had sold them when he needed money. He and other Americans pointed to the sad condition of the nation's 250,000 free blacks to justify not freeing the 1,500,000 blacks who were slaves. She agreed.

Yet some northern Negroes enjoyed their freedom.

Some were even well off. They had educated their children despite the difficulty of finding schools that would take them. In some states—she herself mentioned this fact—black men voted. In New York City, which had probably the largest black community in the North, sixty-six black men had voted in the last election. Yet she could not bring herself to ask for immediate freedom for blacks.

Just before their return to England, Fanny and Camilla visited President James Monroe in the White House. The President was delighted to meet the pretty young ladies who had so many wise and flattering things to say about his country. The conversation turned, as it always did, to the subject on everybody's mind.

"The day is not very far distant," President Monroe told them, "when a slave will not be found in America."

Almost every American who thought about it at all thought that slavery would end of its own accord, some day. Everything would work out. It was just a matter of time.

III
Hands of Steel, Hearts of Flame

It is not every country that is blessed with a Lafayette . . . . Oh, would to Heaven we could X you by 12, and then by the square of 12, and then by the cube of the square, and spread you abroad among the nations of the earth.
FRANCES WRIGHT TO LAFAYETTE

Chapter 9 BEST SELLER

*"The strongest sweetest mind that ever cased
in a human body."*

JEREMY BENTHAM

SHORTLY after their visit with President Monroe, Fanny
and Camilla returned to England. There was special
news in the air that made them anxious and impatient
for the trip to be a quick one: England seemed about to
have a revolution.

When they left for America on the *Amity* two years
earlier there had been a long and bitter strike of the
Manchester spinners. Now Manchester was again in the
news.

The end of the Napoleonic Wars had brought hardship to England. Because the soldiers had come home,
the factories were slowing down. There was no more
need to make uniforms and weapons. Workers were
thrown out of work. The returning soldiers joined the
army of unemployed. The few workers who kept their
jobs worked for miserably low wages.

Low wages had triggered the great strikes in 1818
when the Wright sisters sailed. Now, as they returned,

times were even more desperate. Working people were
in a revolutionary mood.

"Education and starvation have made their way with
the people," Rabina Millar had written to the girls in
America. "Fear [is] making everyone hoard all the silver
they could collect."

There had been strikes and hunger marches. Unemployed workers invaded factories and smashed machin-
ery they thought was taking away their jobs. Hungry
farmworkers paraded and shouted for food. Leaders of
the workers demanded political reforms that would give
them some voice in the government.

In 1819, at a great meeting outside Manchester,
eighty thousand factory workers had crowded into St.
Peter's Field to hear speeches and to sign a giant petition. It was a peaceful meeting. But the government
sent mounted soldiers into the crowd to break it up.
Some people were killed; many more were badly hurt.

The Manchester Massacre (also known as the Pe-
terloo Massacre) almost turned England upside down.
For months there continued to be talk of revolution.

But to Fanny's disgust, by the time she and Camilla
reached England to rejoin Rabina Millar, all the talk
had ended. People were more interested in King
George's divorce. Business had picked up a bit. The
harvest was a good one. The poor had a little more to
eat. There was no more interest in political change.

Fanny returned to her favorite subject—America. In
the summer of 1820 she put her letters to Rabina Millar
in order, selected the best ones, and edited them. Then

she sent the manuscript, *Views of Society and Manners in America,* to a publisher.

Views was an instant best seller. It made Fanny famous. Without this book the world might never have heard of her. It was a book of propaganda extolling the United States. Europeans had almost forgotten about the country across the ocean. They had forgotten about its revolutionary beginnings. If they thought about the United States at all, they thought of it as a distant land filled with radical refugees—or as a place where an enterprising person might make a lot of money. Now Fanny reminded them of the glorious days of Washington and Franklin.

British newspapers and magazines rediscovered America. Liberals and reformers took courage from her enthusiastic description of the American political system. The book proved to them that a people could govern themselves successfully without kings or lords or an established church.

Views was translated into many European languages. All over the continent believers in religious and political liberty were inspired once again by the example of the United States.

Fanny's book counteracted the hostile and sneering picture of America that almost all other European travelers had painted. They had picked out the bad in American life. She had shown what was good.

In the United States the book was very well received. Americans were delighted. She became extremely popular. The *North American Review,* perhaps the leading literary journal in the United States, reported: "It forms, in many respects, a contrast with other works of the same class, and is distinguished for its flattering tone toward our country.

"It has of course its imperfections," the *Review* continued. "The discreet citizen will place it before him as the model toward which he should strive to bring his country, rather than as a tablet of actual perfections."

One of the "imperfections" noted was Fanny's statement that the United States government prohibited the spread of slavery throughout its new territories. "This is true," the *Review* said, "as every American knows, only of the states formed out of the territory northwest of the Ohio." Slavery was not prohibited in much of the Louisiana Purchase.

The Tory magazines in England attacked her book as a slander and an insult to the king and the church. They claimed the author was not an Englishwoman but a male writer hired by radicals to attack the government. Some said the author was an American who hated his mother country. A true Englishwoman, said another magazine, would have blushed at the thought of writing such a book.

Fanny may well have blushed, but it would have been a blush of pride and triumph. The liberal and radical intellectuals took the book to their heart and helped make it a success. When they discovered the author to be a charming young woman in her twenties, they opened their doors to her and made her their heroine.

Jeremy Bentham, the famous old liberal philosopher

who had long admired the United States, wrote, offering Fanny his friendship and the hospitality of his home in Queens Square Place, London.

"I am a single man of seventy," Bentham wrote in his quaint fashion, "but as far from melancholy as a man need be. Hour of dinner six; tea between nine and ten; bed a quarter before eleven."

Bentham's home was famous as a gathering place for most of the leading political philosophers of the time. Although Fanny did not much like social life—she writes about her "strong dislike for all fashionable or other society"—she accepted. She stayed on and off as a guest in the old man's home for a year or two.

She enjoyed the lively philosophical discussions she had with Bentham in the evenings. She called him "her Socrates." She learned much from the many radical thinkers she met there: Francis Place, the trade-union leader and founder of the modern birth-control movement; James Mill, the political economist and historian; John Austin, the liberal legal scholar.

Bentham's philosophy of utilitarianism, which taught that "the greatest good of the greatest number" ought to be the aim of government, had a strong influence on her thinking. The ideas she absorbed at his home reinforced her own brand of Epicureanism.

When Bentham heard that she had written in fictional form a short description of this philosophy while she was a girl in Scotland, he read it and encouraged her to have it published. She did so in 1822, under the title *A Few Days in Athens*. She dedicated the book to Bentham. It added considerably to her growing reputation. An American edition was published a few years later.

But with all her new fame she was moody and restless. Life had no purpose. What should she do with herself? Should she become a writer? Should she continue to travel?

She wrote silly love poetry. One poem she wrote began:

> Where are thy thoughts, my love
> Are they with me?
> Fixed as yon stars above
> Mine are with thee.

She sent it to Harriet Garnett back in America. "You may set these to any air they will fit," she wrote, "and sing them whenever you take to singing."

She expressed doubts about her book *Views.* "You must not expect much from my book . . . . I grow doubtful of my fitness . . . every day."

She hated England. "Do not think me madly prejudiced against this island," she wrote. But she *was* prejudiced. She saw nothing good in England, just as she saw nothing bad in America. Perhaps she associated England with her childhood and the Campbells. They were a bitter memory.

She liked Scotland. She went there on a short visit and found nothing to criticize. In Dundee she met old family servants.

But she was restless, traveling about with faithful

Camilla at her side. She had no one else to love, no cause to take up her passion and her energy.

And then, in the fall of 1821 she received a letter from a famous man.

The Marquis de Lafayette was at sixty-four the most glamorous figure of his time. A vastly wealthy aristocrat, he had joined Washington's army to fight for American freedom. He had become a hero of that war, a man still beloved by those who had fought in the American Revolution. Afterward, he had returned to France to throw in his lot with the French Revolution against the king and his own class.

Now, thirty years later, he was still active in revolutionary politics. He was distrusted in France by the king and the nobles who had come back to power after the defeat of Napoleon. But he was looked to as a leader by French and other European liberals. His wife had died; he lived on his estate at La Grange, about forty miles from Paris, with his two married daughters and their families.

He was especially interested in America. He considered himself an American. As soon as Fanny's book, *Views,* was published, he read it. Then he wrote her a letter of praise. He asked if he could meet her.

Fanny wasted no time setting off for France. On her way to La Grange she stopped in Paris to leave a copy of *Views* with Albert Gallatin, the American ambassador. Gallatin was another historic American figure, a friend of Jefferson's and a member of his cabinet when Jefferson was President.

Gallatin was out of town. He did not meet Fanny personally, but he sent her a note of thanks. He praised her book, remarking that "the liberality which pervades the whole cannot be but very pleasing to the Americans whom former travelers, to say the least, had not much flattered."

Fanny's first visit with Lafayette began as a comedy of errors. While she was on her way to La Grange, he was going in the opposite direction to a political meeting in Paris. When she reached La Grange, she was greeted by the entire Lafayette household, "which comprises three generations," she wrote to Bentham back in London, "sons and daughters with their wives, husbands, and children, to the number, in all, of nineteen." The family was polite, but they did not know what to do with the unexpected young visitor.

Fanny turned right around and rode back to Paris. The following morning she sent a note to Lafayette's hotel. In a few hours the great man himself was at her door.

"Our meeting was scarcely without tears," Fanny wrote. "This venerable friend of human liberty saw in me what recalled to him the most pleasing recollections of his youth (I mean those connected with America)."

What Fanny saw in Lafayette was a revolutionary hero who had not lost his zeal for revolution. He was a slender, distinguished-looking man, about her own height. He wore a blond wig, a blue coat, and ordinary trousers. Over these he wore a great cloak. His manner was quiet but self-confident. He was a man who was used to being obeyed.

He asked her to come to La Grange.

For the next three years she often stayed at the Lafayette estate. He had his private quarters at the top of one of the château's five towers. Directly below, a room was set aside for her use.

She became part of his household. Despite the difference in their ages, they had fallen in love.

Chapter 10 **RETURN TO AMERICA**

"Think of me sometimes—love me always, and drive the left wing out of the Chamber."
FRANCES WRIGHT TO
LAFAYETTE

LAFAYETTE had never met a woman like Fanny. She was not only forceful and intelligent. She was also slender, beautiful, and quite feminine.

The old revolutionary had met other intellectual women, but they had seemed unfeminine.

Ordinary women in his experience were timid and boring. They were unable to talk about anything except their children, household affairs, and the latest gossip. They were dull and uninteresting.

Fanny was a new experience to him. She paid no attention to conventional ideas of how women ought to behave. She loved to discuss politics, and she argued long and eloquently. Her mind was as good as that of any man and better than those of most men he had met. She was able to express her ideas with brilliance and style.

At the same time she always observed the accepted politenesses. Her manner was gracious. She possessed all the proper social skills. She was what the English called a lady.

He was more than twice her age. Yet they loved each other. He may have been the man she loved most in her life.

She wrote him passionate, romantic letters. "You are familiar with all my sentiments," she wrote, "with all my feelings. You know all the thoughts that occupy me. Write to me, my friend, my father. One word will suffice—but let me have that word soon and often."

Fanny would write Lafayette after spending a day in his company, even though she knew she would see him again the next day. "My beloved friend, a thousand thousand thanks for your precious note and your angelic goodness . . . . Tomorrow then, tomorrow I shall see you and bless you again and again for all your goodness to your poor Fanny."

She exerted a strong influence over him. Her one great idea was freedom for all humanity. By this she meant freedom from the power of unjust government, freedom from the power of money, freedom from the power of organized religion. Lafayette seemed to her to be the one man who might help bring such freedom about.

Fanny wanted him to be aggressively radical. She wanted him to lead his liberal and left-wing followers out of the Chamber of Deputies as a protest against King Louis XVIII's reactionary policies.

Lafayette appointed her messenger to the English liberals. But London in the 1820's infuriated her. The English seemed to be totally uninterested in freedom. The government locked people up for having dissenting opinions; yet no one protested very vigorously. She complained to Lafayette about "this dull England." Jeremy Bentham agreed with her. "We need hands of steel and hearts of flame," she said impatiently. What she wanted was revolution in both countries.

The elderly Lafayette was something of a hands-of-steel, heart-of-flame person. He was deeply involved in the plots and conspiracies of the Carbonari. This was a secret revolutionary society with members in many important government posts in France, Spain, and Italy. They were mostly writers and intellectuals dedicated to the overthrow of the reactionary Bourbon kings who came back to power in those countries after the defeat of Napoleon in 1815.

In 1823 the Carbonari were crushed by the French secret police. Members were arrested and jailed for their ideas. Some were shot for plotting revolution, and some of these were close friends of Lafayette's. His position became dangerous. The next year he lost reelection to the Chamber of Deputies, along with many other liberals and radicals. With his political power gone, Lafayette was defenseless. At any moment he might be arrested.

He was also in financial difficulties. He had spent much of his family fortune on politics. He had made some bad investments.

The family at La Grange was becoming hostile to Fanny. They resented her importance in their affairs. They did not think it proper for the old man to spend so much time with her. They were jealous of her.

When she suggested that Lafayette adopt her—he already had two married daughters and an adult son—they were horrified. He himself was rather in favor of the idea. "You know I am your child," she wrote, "the child of your adoption." She called him "my father." He called her "my child, my sweet Fanny."

La Grange now became an uncomfortable place for her to be. Yet Lafayette was unhappy if she was away too long. And Fanny had grown disillusioned with the revolutionaries of Europe. She thought they would *never* free anyone, with their ridiculous secret plots and conspiracies! They seemed romantic and foolish. She labeled their efforts "absurd drawing room intrigue." She called their leaders "fashionable conspirators." Humanity, she decided, would never be liberated by these upper-class adventurers.

At just that moment of crisis and indecision an invitation came from America. It was from President James Monroe and the United States Congress. Would General Lafayette honor the American people by coming to their country as a guest of the nation?

There was no question but that Lafayette would accept. Nor was there much doubt that Fanny and Camilla would also go, but they decided to travel separately. Lafayette left in midsummer; the Wright sisters a month later.

They stepped off their ship onto the pier in New York City almost exactly six years to the day since their first arrival in September 1818.

Much had changed. Instead of an unknown young girl, Fanny was now a famous author. To many Americans she was a national heroine.

The United States had changed, too. Gone was the happy harmony of the Era of Good Feeling. Sharp conflicts and hatreds had arisen in American life. James Monroe was still in the White House, but in November a new president was to be chosen in a bitter political campaign. The candidates were Andrew Jackson of Tennessee, Henry Clay of Kentucky, John Quincy Adams of Massachusetts, and William H. Crawford of Georgia.

Along the Atlantic Coast, in the cities of Wilmington, Baltimore, Philadelphia, New York, and Boston, the seeds of industrialization were sprouting. Where artisans once made shoes, and cut cloth by hand, machines now did much of the work.

Shoemakers, carpenters, and tailors had to abandon their hand tools and their workbenches and their shops for the factories. There they labored long hours for low wages. Even children toiled at machines. Skilled craftsmen became factory hands. They no longer owned their own tools. Now they were dependent on their boss, the manufacturer, the man who owned the machines and paid them wages.

The cities had grown with the factories. New York

now totaled more than 123,000 people. Sixteen hundred new houses were built in the year 1824.

Jefferson had dreamed of an America that would never have large cities, a nation of independent farmers. Now of nine million Americans, close to one million lived in cities.

The nation was growing. It was changing. So were its problems.

With all the changes, Fanny still thought of America as the one country where all things were possible, where one could still experiment, where nothing could stop one from trying new schemes, new ways of living.

She was not at all discouraged.

Wherever Lafayette went, he was greeted by great crowds and celebrations. City after city made him an honorary citizen, declared a holiday, and organized a parade. It is difficult for a modern American to imagine how passionately this French aristocrat was loved.

Old men, veterans of the war of 1776, came out to see the hero in the flesh, Washington's friend and fellow soldier. They idolized him. When they saw him limping from a fall he had taken, they said, "Look! He still limps from his wounds at the Battle of Brandywine!"

Fanny and Camilla followed close behind when they did not travel with him. Some observers—mostly those who disagreed with her politics—were critical. They tried to create a scandal out of the fact that two unmarried young women were traveling with the general.

The Duke of Saxe-Weimar, himself traveling and writing his own book about the new country, was quite sarcastic. He wrote: "This lady, with her sister, unattended by a male protector . . . constantly tagged about after General Lafayette, and whenever the General arrived at any place, Miss Wright was sure to follow the next day . . . . The flattering terms in which she speaks of Americans and all their institutions are regarded as overstrained."

Lafayette spent a good part of his time visiting old friends. Fanny was delighted to accompany him. She enjoyed the intellectual excitement of talking with such wise old men as Thomas Jefferson, James Madison, and John Adams.

For their part these men looked upon Fanny as a promise that their ideas would survive into the future. She appeared to them like a bright young soldier, carrying on the revolution they had begun.

When he heard that Fanny was traveling with Lafayette, Jefferson invited them to Monticello to see the achievement he was most proud of, the University of Virginia at Charlottesville. Boasting of his university, he talked of the importance of education. "Who knows," he wrote, "by what future Miss Wright . . . the world may some day be gratified and instructed."

At Monticello Fanny talked with Jefferson about slavery. She found him worried. He was hopeful that slavery would be abolished at least in Virginia, if not throughout the South. He worried about a future war between blacks seeking their freedom and whites resisting.

Fanny did not disagree. She too feared that war. She did not believe that blacks could ever live peacefully among white Americans. Whites, she thought, were too frightened of the possibility of racial intermarriage.

She wrote to friends in Europe: "The prejudice, whether absurd or the contrary, against the mixture of the two colors is so deeply rooted in the American mind that emancipation without expatriation (if indeed the word be applicable) seems impossible." She knew that Jefferson and Madison and all the other planters she had met hoped that freed slaves would leave or be taken out of the country. Fortunately, she added, there was the black republic of Haiti nearby. American blacks were welcome there.

There was no hint in her thinking that slavery was wrong. She saw it only as a problem for her beloved America. She was not much more sensitive to the wishes and feelings of the blacks than were Jefferson and other planters.

In Washington, after their stay at Monticello, Fanny and Camilla sat in the gallery and watched Lafayette formally received by the Senate. The Washington *Gazette* noted that among the ladies present were "the celebrated English authoress, Miss Wright, and her sister."

Two weeks later, Congress gave Lafayette two hundred thousand dollars and a large tract of land in recognition of his services to the American people. He invested more than half the money in United States savings bonds.

Fanny and Camilla often listened to congressional debates. Fanny was educating herself about the actual workings of the American government. During recesses, congressmen crowded around the young ladies. In those days few women ever attended a congressional session. She and Camilla were a novelty.

She was interested in more than partisan politics. Congress was quarreling over who should be President —Andrew Jackson or John Quincy Adams—because neither candidate had won a majority of electoral votes. But Fanny was concerned with deeper questions.

How should people live? How could this new society produce a better human being? In what way might America show the rest of the world the way to freedom?

Chapter 11 SLAVERY

*"An impartial spectator opens his eyes
in amazement at this wonderful attachment to a pure white skin—the purity
of which the climate destroys before
the age of five and twenty."*

FRANCES WRIGHT

THE slavery of the blacks began to concern her. It
seemed to be America's greatest problem, the one great
defect of the American experiment.

The short trip to Virginia with Lafayette had given
her a brief firsthand look at slavery. Instead of a word
on paper, she now saw men, women, and children
shackled like animals and whipped as they were driven
up the gangplank of a ship to be taken to Savannah.
The blacks were things. The whites with the whips were
brutish monsters. The whole spectacle revolted her.

Fanny went back to the library and studied the laws
regulating slavery. She visited planters near Washington
and asked them about how slavery affected young white
people who were taught to consider themselves the masters of other human beings. They discussed with her the

economic advantages and disadvantages of slavery. She compared its productivity with that of free labor.

But she still knew little about it. All she knew was what she had read in books or heard in pleasant living rooms. To really understand it, she would have to travel extensively through all the South.

Harriet Garnett, now living in England, tried to dissuade her. Slavery, she wrote, was too horrible, too awful for a lady's eyes. But Fanny wanted to see for herself. In the spring of 1825 she left Lafayette, and with Camilla journeyed south and west to New Orleans.

She found the conditions of slavery grew harsher and harsher the farther south she traveled. The inhumanity and the immorality of owning human beings, of buying and selling them, sickened her. She described slavery as "this horrible ulcer which now covers a large half of this magnificent country." And she saw it at its most horrible in the slave-trading city of New Orleans.

"I expected to find it here in all its horrors," she wrote, "and truly in all its horrors is it found."

She walked past the slave market and saw human flesh peddled from the block. The blacks stood naked in chains. The auctioneer bellowed their ages and prices— and their special skills. The white slave buyers walked up to the human property, prodded mouths open to see how healthy teeth were, felt muscles, pinched flesh.

She saw a black woman bought by one master and dragged away at the end of a rope, weeping, while her twelve-year-old daughter remained behind to be sold to some other master.

She and Camilla could hardly speak for shame. They walked back to their hotel through the muddy, mosquito-ridden streets. They passed slave jails, where blacks were chained by neck and ankle, their hands tied behind them.

"And for what?" she asked. "For disputing the will of some iron-hearted tyrant! For having tried to run away!"

She noted that "every man's hand is against the slave." Anyone with a white skin could stop and question anyone with a black skin, even if the black was free. A runaway slave could be arrested by any white man.

Fanny was shocked to learn the story of the free blacks in the war of 1812. When the British attacked New Orleans, many free blacks had volunteered to serve in Andrew Jackson's army. They were welcomed, and they fought bravely and well. But after the American victory their guns were taken from them, and they were forbidden to carry arms again. They were treated with hatred and contempt by the whites. From Andrew Jackson down, whites feared free blacks and hoped they would go away—preferably to some other country.

Fanny found slavery brutal and degrading not only to the blacks. It made many whites ignorant, lazy, and stupid. Whites in the South did not seem to her to be able to think intelligently. This was because they considered themselves a master race and found no need to think hard or work hard. "An impartial spectator opens his eyes in amazement," she observed, "at this wonderful attachment to a pure white skin . . . ."

She decided that slavery must be abolished. The slaves must be freed. There were, she had heard Jefferson say, about 1,500,000 slaves. On their labor rested much of the social and economic system of the United States. They represented an important part of the wealth of the country.

How could one free the slaves—deprive owners of their property—without destroying the United States? Did not the United States Constitution protect the right of a man to do as he pleased with his own property?

Jefferson, Madison, and Monroe had owned slaves. Many of the men of 1776 had owned slaves. Even Benjamin Franklin had once owned a black slave.

Yet these men had led the revolution and founded a free republic dedicated to the belief that all men were created equal. It was the *institution* of slavery that was horrible, not the slaveowners.

Many of the Virginia and Maryland planters she met despised slavery. They were anxious to see it disappear. Some had freed their own slaves.

Jefferson himself had said he feared for the future of the country if slavery did not end. Blacks would not remain slaves forever. There had been violent slave revolts. Only three years earlier black Denmark Vesey had been caught planning a slave revolt in South Carolina. What would happen to the world's bright dream of freedom if the United States perished one day in a bloody racial war?

The strange thing was that none of these wise old men—philosophers, former Presidents, even Lafayette —could think of a peaceful solution to the problem. All they could do was hope.

Fanny was certain that any worthwhile solution would have to be peaceful. It would have to take into consideration not only the slaves but their owners. The owners would have to be paid for the loss of their property. The slaves would have to be helped, or they would not long be able to keep and enjoy their freedom.

Fanny grew thoughtful. Slavery was not something to be ended easily, without a great deal of planning.

Some scheme would have to be devised, she decided, that would make the end of slavery acceptable to the slaveowners.

And some system must be found to prepare the blacks for freedom.

Chapter 12 ALL THINGS
IN COMMON

*"That which you propose is well worthy of
trial. It has succeeded with certain portions
of our white brethren under the care of a
Rapp and an Owen; and why may it not succeed with the man of color?"*
THOMAS JEFFERSON TO
FRANCES WRIGHT

AFTER her southern trip Fanny traveled through the
West to visit the communal settlements she had heard
about in Pennsylvania and Indiana. She was also interested in visiting the commune set up at New Harmony,
Indiana, by the Englishman Robert Owen. And there
was another commune she wanted to have a look at in
Illinois. All these experimental communities were socialist, or communist. No private property was allowed.
Everyone worked together and shared together.

All sorts of experiments in communist living were
being tried in America in the early nineteenth century.
It was as if, by getting rid of their king, Americans had

announced to the idealists of the world: *Come and try your schemes here for a new way of life!*

Many of the pioneers in communal living were pious Christians. The Shakers set up communities in which all property was held in common. There were many other such religious sects.

The Rappites were the best known and most successful. They took their name from that of their founder and leader, George Rapp. He had brought them over from Württemburg, Germany, in the year 1804. They were poor Lutheran peasants who believed literally in the Biblical verse: "And the multitude of them that believed were of one heart and one soul; neither said any of them that aught of the things he possessed was his own, but they had all things in common."

None of the Rappites owned anything; all property, including personal possessions, was owned by the commune. They drank only water, wore rough clothes. All the wealth they produced went into the common treasury. They exalted work, prayer, and simplicity.

The Rappites were extremely successful. Their farms were rich and productive. Their commune was able to accumulate a good deal of money.

Fanny and Camilla spent a few days at their new settlement at Economy, Pennsylvania. They listened with pleasure to the singing of the Rapp children. Fanny discussed the organization of commune life with the eldest son, Becker Rapp.

But she soon decided that the Rapp commune was no

paradise. George Rapp ruled his people like an iron-handed dictator. There was no freedom, no democracy. He alone decided what education the children should receive. He alone controlled all the wealth the community produced.

The fields, orchards, and gardens were well cared for. The horses and cattle were fat and healthy. The crops were rich and brought a good price. Everyone had enough to eat. Since the Rappites denied themselves everything but the simplest necessities of life, the treasury was filled with gold and silver.

But Fanny thought: "Where were the great and beautiful works of art, or libraries, or laboratories, or scientific workshops . . . ? Where were the children trained to excellence by the spur of emulation . . . ?"

Life in the Rapp commune was grim and joyless. Everyone played his part like an ant in an anthill. Fanny decided that a cooperative society ought to be more democratic. It ought to create beauty. It should encourage scientific habits of thinking rather than religious superstition.

Another cooperative settlement had been set up at Albion, in Edwards County in southeast Illinois, by Morris Birkbeck and George Flower. They were rich English Quakers. The members of their commune were English farmers fleeing from hunger and poverty.

The Albion commune was not religious but political in nature. Its members believed in democracy and were strongly antislavery. Under the leadership of George, they went to the polls in 1823 and helped defeat a new constitution that would have made Illinois a slave state. Young George Flower knew Lafayette. He had visited him on his way to America in 1814. The general had given him a letter of introduction to Jefferson, and the former President thereafter took a fatherly interest in George.

George Flower was an unusual man: he not only held strong opinions against slavery, he actually did something to help black people.

He rented some of the Albion lands to free blacks. When kidnappers tried to capture them and take them south down the Wabash River to be sold into slavery in Kentucky, Flower defended the blacks and gave them weapons. When it became clear that free black farmers could not survive in a sea of white hostility, he made arrangements to have them go to the independent black republic of Haiti.

At his own expense he sent twenty-five black families to settle there. Haitian President Jean Pierre Boyer gave them farms on his own land. Flower later received a formal document of appreciation from the black president.

Flower suffered for this. The white neighbors of the Albion commune hated him for taking up the cause of the blacks and giving them arms. One of them murdered his son, Richard. The man who did it was tried and acquitted. The jury made it clear they would have liked to have rewarded the murderer.

Fanny had firsthand experience of the terror a free black faced. While riding alone in the country near Albion, she came upon a young black man with his hands tied, being dragged along the road by a band of white men. They were taking him in the direction of the Wabash River six miles away.

Fanny wheeled her horse and dashed back to Albion. There she got some farmers to help her. They rode back as fast as they could, but by the time they caught up the kidnappers and the young black man were in Kentucky. The farmers jumped from their horses and attacked the kidnappers. Fanny untied the young man's hands. Then they took him to the sheriff, who promised to protect him for the night while Fanny and her friends found a place to sleep.

"The next morning," Fanny told a friend later, "everyone had disappeared, and the sheriff seemed to know nothing about it . . . . I must always accuse myself for having given way to fatigue and . . . [left] the task of guarding him to others."

This experience convinced her that blacks must have protection and help to get and keep their freedom. They could not depend solely on the law. One should not turn slaves free and leave them defenseless in the midst of a world of white enemies. This conviction strongly influenced Fanny's thinking about the emancipation of slaves.

It was probably Robert Owen who gave her the idea of solving the problem by means of a commune. Owen had been successful in the cotton-spinning business in England and Scotland. He had become a millionaire.

Owen was an unusual factory owner. In his mill at New Lanark, Scotland, he had experimented with ways of improving the working conditions of his employees. In other mills the employer was concerned only with working his laborers as hard as he could for as long as he could—so that he could make as much money as possible out of their labor.

But Owen was a humanitarian and a reformer. In his factory, men, women, and children worked ten and a half hours a day. In other factories they worked twelve or thirteen hours.

In those days poor children were treated worse than horses and cattle, certainly much worse than pet cats and dogs. There were no laws limiting the number of hours they might work or providing them with an education. Children as young as five years of age would start working in factories and mines and slave their lives away operating machines. They never went to school.

Owen would not employ children younger than twelve years of age. And he established a school for those children who did work in his mills, hiring teachers for them with his own money. This was an unheard-of act of generosity and earned for him a reputation as a radical.

In his mills wages were somewhat lower than those paid in other mills. But when his mills were idle, Owen continued to pay his workers full wages, instead of discharging them, as his competitors did. And yet Owen made a great deal of money.

He was a strange sort of capitalist. He was convinced

that capitalism was bad because it required men to compete with each other. He believed that competition was the source of all evil. It made men greedy and selfish. It made it impossible for people to love each other and to live in harmony.

Owen believed that men could be free and happy only if they lived in a cooperative socialist society. He wanted to build a model of such a society. This would show the world the advantages of cooperative living.

Owen's ideas had found a ready welcome in the United States. Its leaders—men like Jefferson, Madison, and Monroe—were receptive to his philosophy. They, too, wanted to make a better world. To many Americans of the 1820's, Owen's ideas seemed a way by which their country might avoid the poverty, crime, and misery that industrial progress was bringing to England.

In late 1824, Owen visited the successful Rappite settlement at Harmony, Indiana. Shortly after New Year's Day he bought the settlement. The Rappites moved to Economy. In the spring of 1825 Owen came to Washington and lectured on his ideas before Congress. Among his listeners were outgoing President Monroe and incoming President John Quincy Adams.

Fanny sat and listened, too. What he said made sense to her.

In Owen's model community everyone would work, and no one would starve. The commune would grow and manufacture all it needed and sell the rest. The sale of these surplus products would provide income for the entire community to share.

Instead of going into the pockets of a single individual as profit, this extra income would be spent on schools, libraries, and hospitals—on things for everyone to use and enjoy. The idea that labor created surplus wealth, and that the wealth should be used for the good of all, instead of going to enrich the capitalist owner, has led many writers to label Robert Owen the first socialist.

If men grew up in a noncompetitive socialist world, said Owen, they would be kind and friendly. There would be no more war. There would be no more hatred. There would be no more poverty.

There was one part of Owen's thinking that may have puzzled Fanny. His socialism was for white people only. Like many others, he was prejudiced against blacks.

In his constitution for the Society of New Harmony, Owen wrote: "Persons of all ages and descriptions, exclusive of color, may become members . . . . Persons of color may be received as helpers to the Society, if necessary; or if it be found useful, to prepare and enable them to become associates in communities in Africa; or in some other country; or in some other part of this country . . . ."

When he talked of humanity Owen meant only white humanity. One must conclude that he did not consider black people fully human.

Fanny thought: Could not a cooperative society be a halfway house between slavery and freedom? If slaves could be placed in their own New Harmony with the prospect of working for their freedom, might they not work harder? And would they not therefore produce a surplus of wealth, just as the Rappites did, a surplus that could be used to pay their masters for their freedom?

Fanny considered the financial success of the Rappites. Why could not the same success be achieved by a commune of slaves? There was not much difference, she said, "in the intellectual advancement between the mass of the German laborers . . . submitted to the . . . control of astute leaders, and that of the southern Negro."

She was an earnest student. All through her western trip she thought about her plan for emancipation by means of a commune. At Albion she talked to George Flower. He and his wife were enthusiastic. He offered to sell half his property and put the money into such a commune.

When she rejoined Lafayette and discussed the subject with him, he was encouraging. His reaction became especially favorable when he learned that she intended, after the slaves were trained, to set them free outside the United States.

She asked Lafayette to raise the question with his important friends. She wanted active support. She herself sent letters describing her plan to Thomas Jefferson and other prominent Americans.

Jefferson, too, was in favor. "The abolition of the evil [slavery]," he wrote back, "is not impossible; it ought never to be despaired of. Every plan should be adopted, every experiment tried, which do something towards the ultimate object. That which you propose is well worthy of trial. It has succeeded with certain portions of our white brethren, under the care of a Rapp and an Owen; and why may it not succeed with the men of color?"

Jefferson was ill. He had not left his house for months. Active support was out of the question. "With one foot in the grave and the other lifted to follow it," he told Fanny, "I do not permit myself to take part in any enterprise, even for bettering the condition of man . . . ." He wished her every success.

She went to Baltimore to see Benjamin Lundy, editor and publisher of *The Genius of Universal Emancipation.* Lundy, a Quaker born the same year as the French Revolution, was one of America's first abolitionists. He traveled up and down the land preaching against slavery.

Lundy could see no future for the black man in the United States. He was constantly on the lookout for places where freed slaves might settle. Haiti, Texas (then a part of Mexico), and Africa attracted his attention.

The idea of settling black people in another country was popular with whites who did not like slavery but who also did not like to have black neighbors. Some slaveowners encouraged colonization as a scheme for getting rid of old sick slaves who could neither work nor be sold for much money. Colonization took the expense of feeding and caring for such slaves off their hands.

Some influential white people had set up the American Colonization Society. The society tried to get public funds to be used for settling black people in Africa. In 1822 it founded the African country of Liberia for this purpose. Its capital, Monrovia, was named after President James Monroe, a leading supporter of the Colonization Society.

The society did not encourage free blacks to go to Haiti, which had been an independent black nation since 1795. Haiti was too close to the United States. Slaveowners did not much like the idea of calling the attention of millions of American blacks to the successful black revolution that had taken place there.

But President Boyer of Haiti welcomed American black settlers. He was especially anxious to attract strong young farmers and workers like the people George Flower had brought over.

Free black Americans had mixed feelings about colonization. Some had gone to Liberia and found it a great disappointment. Others had prospered there. One of the earliest black newspapers in the United States, *The Rights of All,* thought colonization might be of some value to the handful of American blacks "that might emigrate and survive.

"But as it respects the millions that are now in the United States," the paper continued, "and the eight millions that in twenty or twenty-five years will be in this country, we think it is in no way calculated to meet their wants or ameliorate their condition."

A few months later, the paper's editor and publisher, Reverend Samuel E. Cornish, warned his readers: "By no means go to Africa . . . . We conceive of no enemy

of the colored people of this country so formidable as
the 'colonization society.' "

Black independent Haiti was another matter. *The
Rights of All* commented favorably on the emancipation
and settlement there of twelve former slaves from Maryland.

Fanny wanted support for her commune from all
people, northern as well as southern, conservative as
well as radical. She wanted support from people like
George Flower and also from people like President
Monroe.

She wrote up her plan in pamphlet form, and in September 1825, Benjamin Lundy published it. It was entitled *A Plan for the Gradual Abolition of Slavery in the
United States Without Danger of Loss to the Citizens of
the South.* A few weeks later Robert Owen's weekly, the
New Harmony Gazette, reprinted it.

It called for the purchase of land in the South where
crops like tobacco and cotton—crops known to be suitable for slave labor—could be grown. It also called for
the purchase of from fifty to a hundred slaves.

The slaves were to work the land. They would form
part of a commune in which all would share alike. They
would be supervised by the leaders of the commune.
After working long enough to pay back, through their
labor, their purchase price plus 6 percent interest, they
would be set free. Fanny estimated that this would take
about five years for the average black worker.

While this plan of Fanny's was attractive to many
white people, it could not have appealed to blacks. Why

should they have to work off their "purchase" price?
Their labor had been stolen from them. They had not
been paid for it. They had not been asked if they
wanted to be "purchased." No one had asked their
opinion of the plan.

Fanny did not seek the approval or disapproval of
blacks. She discussed it only with whites—some of
whom, like Lundy, were well meaning; others were not.
There is no record in any of the books or newspapers
published by blacks of their reaction to the plan. If they
read of it in Lundy's paper, they probably thought of it
as one more "colonization" scheme to rid the United
States of free blacks.

Fanny did not spell out in print exactly where the
blacks would live when they received their freedom.
"Independent of Haiti," she wrote, "there is the Mexi-
can territory of Texas." She also suggested United
States territory beyond the Rocky Mountains.

In the back of her mind was the hope that black
slaves leaving the South would be replaced by white
workers from the North, who would then become farm
workers, and eventually farmers owning their own land.
Thus she hoped at one stroke to end black chattel slavery, in which workers were owned as property, and
white wage slavery, in which factory workers were
forced to work very long hours for very little money.
This was a highly impractical idea. Slavery came into
existence in the first place because planters could not
afford to pay wages to the great numbers of laborers
needed to work on their plantations.

An important part of the commune was to be the school. It was to be similar to the school set up by Owen for the education of the children working in his factories. Black children would be taught to read and write. One night a week all adults would attend a class for their own education.

Fanny was an ardent believer in education. She was convinced it was the only way to change people, to make them better. She was anxious to turn unskilled slave laborers into skilled workers. She wanted to increase the productivity of black labor.

White people approved of her plan. Slave-owning General Andrew Jackson thought well of it. Former President James Monroe approved. Abolitionist Benjamin Lundy and George Flower were also in favor of it.

The basic assumption of the plan was that blacks could never live freely among whites. Jackson believed that, as did Flower and Lundy. Fanny believed it, too. She kept to herself her private hope that some day free blacks and whites would intermarry, and so end America's race problem once and for all.

From its very beginning, then, it was a white plan. It took no heed of black people's feelings. It did not consult them. This was its great weakness. Blacks could not be expected to cooperate if they had no voice, no vote, no power.

More important to Fanny than the support of American whites was the support she received from Lafayette. She and Camilla rejoined him at Pittsburgh and discussed the plan with him in detail.

At first he was upset by the news that they would not
return with him to Europe. But he soon realized that
they could not really remain with him. His family was
too jealous, and was raising too many objections. He
himself had important interests that did not concern
Fanny. It was also apparent to him that Fanny's heart
would remain in the United States. The reform of
America was becoming a serious passion to her.

Lafayette agreed that Haiti was the best place to re-
settle blacks after they received their freedom. He had
always felt a special loyalty to the French-speaking
black island republic. That was why he had brought
George Flower and Haitian President Boyer together
and had encouraged the earlier resettlement there of
Flower's black farmer friends from Illinois.

One problem worried the general. How could Fanny
and Camilla be protected from violence? The average
southern white objected to any scheme that looked as if
it might educate blacks. In some states it was against the
law to teach a black child to read and write.

Fanny convinced Lafayette that such laws would give
her no trouble. With the support of such important people as Jackson and Jefferson, and now even Governor
De Witt Clinton of New York, she would be secure.
"Also," she added, "I am very generally known and
looked upon as a friend by the American people." As to
violence, she thought "my very sex might be a defense."

While the old revolutionary hero listened to her
forceful arguments, he could see a change had come
over Fanny. She was still fond of him, but she had

found something else to love, a purpose to spend her life on. It was questionable whether Fanny could ever love any person as much as she could love a cause she believed in.

She wrote a long letter to the Garnetts in England, and told them why she was staying in America and would not be seeing them again soon. "If you knew all the horrors connected with southern slavery . . . the ruin with which it threatens this country—its sin, its suffering, its disgrace—you would rejoice, dear loves, in our loss, since I so think it promises fair to pave the way for the destruction of this monster."

She and Lafayette said farewell.

IV
Nashoba

I, Frances Wright, do hereby give the lands after specified . . . in perpetual trust for the benefit of the Negro race.

DEED OF NASHOBA

Chapter 13 FANNY WRIGHT'S COMMUNE

"This establishment is founded on the principle of community of property and labor."

FRANCES WRIGHT

IN October 1825, Fanny bought a large tract of land from representatives of Andrew Jackson.

She had ridden on horseback all around Memphis. With the help of George Flower she was looking for good cotton soil. They wanted it to be in the uplands, to avoid the fever plagues that swept the fertile river valleys every summer. She finally found the place for her experiment. It was about thirteen miles up the Wolf River from Memphis. To this land, bought from Jackson, Fanny later added enough property to bring the total to some two thousand acres.

She bought it with her own money. She invested more of her fortune in tools, in the building of cabins, and later in the purchase of slaves to bring to the commune. In all she spent eight thousand dollars. George Flower's contribution was two thousand dollars' worth of food and livestock.

In a letter in Benjamin Lundy's paper she described the land as "two thousand acres of good and pleasant woodland, traversed by a clear and lovely stream." In another part of the letter she calls it "dry, rolling, and second-rate soil. I trust we shall secure health . . . . The soil and climate are well suited to cotton, and will admit also of good northern farming."

She called the place Nashoba, after the old Chickasaw word for wolf. She invited antislavery people to come and join her in her great experiment.

George Flower went back to Albion to prepare his family and Camilla to move to Nashoba in the spring of 1826. Agents in Nashville were instructed to purchase slaves. Fanny stayed on to supervise the construction of cabins and barns.

Often that winter she wrote to old friends in England and France. "Here I am at last," she wrote to one young woman she had met at Lafayette's home, "propertyowner in the forests of this new territory, bought from the Indians by the United States about five years ago and still inhabited by bears, wolves, and panthers.

"I have traveled the length and breadth of this territory two times, doing forty miles a day on horseback, through unbroken country, spending the night in cabins open to the air on all sides, or in the woods themselves, a bearskin for my bed, my saddle for a pillow.

"Behold me . . . waiting for my friends from Illinois and my Negroes from Nashville. In the meantime I am overseeing the construction of houses on my land with a well which furnishes very good water. All these small matters keep me very busy, for there is nothing more difficult than to make men work in these parts."

It was indeed difficult to make men work in those rough forests of western Tennessee. In that one sentence, Fanny described the key to Nashoba's future troubles.

In February, before the arrival of the Flowers and Camilla, a slaveowner with six slaves turned up unexpectedly from South Carolina. He had read about the commune in Benjamin Lundy's paper. He had seen the invitation to planters who wished to free their slaves but could not afford the expense.

So he had traveled six hundred miles in order to present Fanny with a pregnant black woman and five small black girls. The six were in no condition to do much productive work. Right at the outset the commune would have to meet the expense of caring for them without gaining any benefit from their labor. Nevertheless, Fanny welcomed them and paid the planter his expenses as promised. It came to $446.76. She agreed in writing to prepare the slaves for freedom and to free them in fifteen years or sooner. She promised to settle them in Haiti, Mexico, or Liberia.

A few weeks later the Flowers and Camilla arrived from Albion with food, supplies, and farm tools. Two days later a slave dealer brought eight blacks from Nashville and sold them to Fanny. Five were men; three were women. Their names were Willis, Jacob,

Grandison, Redick, Henry, Nelly, Peggy, and Kitty. The cheapest of them cost five hundred dollars; the most expensive fifteen hundred.

A careful accounting was begun. Each slave would be charged with his purchase price. He was also to be charged for the cost of the food he ate and the clothing he was given. All the hours of work he performed would be recorded to his credit. Any extra work he did, or any special labor, was also to be entered to his credit.

When the credits of a slave equaled the charges for his purchase plus 6 percent interest, his food, and his clothing, he was to be set free. Thus the slaves were to buy their freedom with their labor.

It was now fast approaching spring-planting time. An enormous amount of hard work would have to be done if a crop was to be planted in time to produce something for market in the fall. If a good crop could be raised, Nashoba would have earned some income in its first year.

First, trees would have to be cut down, and their stumps pulled. Rocks and boulders must be dug out of the soil. The earth would have to be broken and turned for cultivation, then plowed and seeded. To do the job there was Fanny, Camilla, George, and the adult slaves. The pregnant woman and the five little girls might help in chores around the cabins, but they could hardly do heavy farm work, nor could Mrs. Flower or her three small children.

It rained almost constantly that spring. When the rain

stopped, a sickly hot yellow sun came out and turned
the land into a steaming oven. The Flower children
suffered from the dampness and the heat. Camilla fell
sick.

The food was rough and poor. There were no fresh
vegetables, no fresh meat. There was no milk, no fruit,
no sugar. The corn bread was coarse and tasteless.

They slept on damp, ill-made beds in drafty cabins.
Some of the cabins had leaky roofs, and the rain came
through while they slept.

In April Camilla and the Flower children returned to
Albion. Fanny's spirits stayed high. She spent days in
the saddle, riding from one end of Nashoba to the
other. But actually she was not feeling well, either.

She did not neglect education. The school had not yet
been built. She had not found a teacher. But she did institute weekly meetings with the slaves. At these meetings she tried to instruct them in philosophy and science. She thought this was necessary to prepare them
for freedom.

She explained the workings of the Nashoba plan to
them. She informed them that although they could not
leave the commune, and although they had to work
each day, they were no longer property.

It must have been extremely difficult to explain this to
them. From their point of view it seemed as if they were
still slaves, despite what she said. Had they not been
bought for money? Were they not forced to work?

They were not treated the way slaves were usually

treated. There was no whipping, no threats of violence. George Flower did not beat them. He simply met them every morning and told them the tasks of the day.

But they still felt like slaves and worked like slaves, and in fact they *were* slaves. They had been bought. They saw no reason to work for these new masters. For they looked upon Fanny and George as masters, not as friends.

Fanny's plan for a self-sufficient commune required highly skilled, hard-working members in order to be successful. The Rapp commune was highly successful; but it was run by George Rapp's iron hand. And the Rappites were held together and motivated to work hard by their religious fanaticism.

For Fanny's commune to be successful—for Robert Owen's commune at New Harmony to be successful— the members would have to be as disciplined and as hard-working as the Rappite Germans. At neither Nashoba nor New Harmony was this the case. At Nashoba, with unskilled and unmotivated black slaves, supervised by easy-going and inexperienced overseers like Fanny and George Flower, success looked far away that first rainy spring.

By May, fifteen acres had been cleared for corn; two acres had been planted in cotton; and a five-acre apple orchard started. A potato patch had also been planted. But the month of May was extremely late for planting. They would be lucky if they had any crop at all. It was unlikely that whatever crops they did raise would bring any extra income into the treasury.

By May they had also found a third white member for Nashoba. He was James Richardson, a Scotsman Fanny had met in Memphis. He shared her passion for philosophy. He had the same opinions with regard to religion. He, too, did not think much of marriage. Like Fanny, he objected to any human relationship regulated by the force of law. They were like-minded people.

Richardson was a useful addition to the commune. He had studied medicine in Edinburgh. His presence would give Nashoba the closest thing to a doctor they could find. He had also been trained as a bookkeeper, and he would be able to keep accurate records of the slaves' accounts, as well as of Nashoba's finances.

In May, feeling sick, tired out by the long months of hard labor, Fanny left Nashoba to rejoin Camilla. She was relieved to think that Richardson would help George Flower keep an eye on things in her absence.

She did not stay at Albion. She and Camilla set out on horseback for New Harmony. She had heard of the many interesting young people there. Perhaps she would find recruits for Nashoba among them.

Chapter 14 NEW HARMONY

*"Her vigorous character, rare cultivation and hopeful
enthusiasm gradually gave her great influence over
me . . . . we became intimate friends."*

ROBERT DALE OWEN

ROBERT OWEN'S eldest son, Robert Dale Owen, was a
young man in his early twenties when Frances Wright
came riding into New Harmony in the spring of 1826.
She burst into his life like a beautiful rocket from the
strange, rare world of his father.

Six years older than he was, she was, he later recalled,
"a tall commanding figure, somewhat slender and
graceful, though her shoulders were a little bit too high;
a face . . . though delicately chiselled, was masculine
rather than feminine; . . . the forehead broad but not
high; the short chestnut hair curling naturally all over a
classic head; the large, blue eyes not soft, but clear and
earnest."

She must have seemed a fascinating ambassador from
the glittering world of London and Paris to that little
backwoods American community. She spoke French
and Italian, was an intimate friend of the great Lafa-

yette, and knew personally all the European radicals and reformers. She had met Jefferson, Jackson, Madison, and Monroe. She had lived in Jeremy Bentham's house. She was the well-known author of not one but two books, as well as a play.

Most important, thought Robert Dale Owen, "she was ready to make great sacrifices to carry out her convictions. Her rare cultivation and hopeful enthusiasm gradually gave her great influence over me . . . ."

Writing many years later, when he was an old man, he apologized for his radical youth. He also insisted he and Fanny had never been lovers. "Friends," he said, "but never . . . anything more. . . . While I saw much to admire in Frances Wright, I found nothing to love."

But that was not how he felt in the years immediately after their first meeting. At that time he was entirely dominated by Fanny's charm and personality. They traveled to Europe together. He became a leading member of her commune in Tennessee. When she moved to New York to edit her famous newspaper, the *Free Enquirer*, he moved with her to help edit it.

It would be hard to say which influenced the other more. Although he suggests she changed his life, she herself picked up and adopted many of his ideas and those of his famous father. There is reason to believe that he hoped to marry her some day. She was fond of him, and she felt responsible for him. Fanny's emotions were a mixture of womanly love and big-sisterly affection.

Dale (that was what Fanny called him) was a bright

young man with a great deal of idealism in his make up. He had just completed his education at a private school in Switzerland. Fanny's young cousin, James Mylne, had been his classmate. Now he had come to Indiana to live the life of backwoods socialism in his father's commune.

Dale was not handsome. He was short, with small eyes and a large mouth. But he was friendly and charming. Most important, in Fanny's eyes, he shared many of her opinions. He was interested in all the radical ideas that swirled around New Harmony. He also found time to enjoy the dances and concerts that were held in the New Harmony meeting hall.

Fanny told Dale how much impressed she was with the weekly newspaper published there. He was one of the editors of the *New Harmony Gazette.* She knew that he contributed articles to it. She praised his forthrightness and his clear style of writing. Dale was a good writer and a careful editor.

The *Gazette* was a lively paper. It reprinted Mary Wollstonecraft's *A Vindication of the Rights of Woman.* It took a forthright liberal, if not radical, position on every political issue of the day.

While Fanny was at New Harmony, the *Gazette* commented favorably on Maryland's "Jew Bill." This was a law that changed the state constitution to permit non-Christians to hold public office and to practice law. It had taken ten years of bitter political struggle in Maryland to get such a bill passed.

Both Fanny and Dale favored it, but not because

they had special sympathies for Jews. They objected to governmental interference in religious belief. Like his father, Dale was bitterly antireligious. He considered all religions, including the Jewish religion, no better than superstition. He encouraged Fanny in her own antireligious tendencies.

She found his intellectual courage attractive. "She told me," he wrote, "that I was one of the few persons she had ever met with whom she felt that in her reformatory efforts she could act in unison."

He was not the only young man who fell under the spell of the beautiful Wrights. Camilla's conquest was a gentle young man named Richesson Whitby. He had come to New Harmony from a pious Shaker commune further east, where he had been the overseer. The quiet, religious atmosphere of Shaker life had not prepared young Whitby for the intellectual excitement of the Owen commune, where radical ideas were bounced back and forth across the dining-room table like tennis balls.

Richesson was a little afraid of Fanny. But he found Camilla tender and sympathetic. Camilla was younger; Camilla was gentler. She suited shy Richesson. He must have suited her, for they fell in love.

Another young member of the New Harmony commune was tough-looking Robert Jennings, a former minister who had left a wife and children somewhere back East. He, too, was an editor of the *Gazette*. What he most loved to do was to teach school. Although he was no longer a clergyman, Jennings enjoyed lecturing.

He was a practical-minded, well-organized thinker. He could argue forcefully and well. He was a good man to have around when one wanted to get things done.

There were many other people at New Harmony, some of them older. One in particular attracted Fanny's attention. He was William Phiquepal D'Arusmont, a short, middle-aged Frenchman, an educational reformer who had come over from France to set up a progressive school.

D'Arusmont had revolutionary ideas about education. He believed that it should be useful, that school should teach young people practical subjects that would fit them for an occupation. He had brought three French boys with him to Indiana, and there at Owen's commune with their help he taught some sixty boys mathematics, spelling, and other useful skills.

For all these people, and for all the other members of the New Harmony community, Fanny and Camilla had exciting news of the progress of their experiment at Nashoba. One would never have guessed that the two young women had come to Indiana to rest from their difficult labors and to recuperate from illness brought on by overwork.

Chapter 15 A SECOND REVOLUTION

"Man, up to this hour, has been in all parts of the world, a slave to a trinity of the most monstrous evils that could be combined to inflict mental and physical evil upon his whole race. I refer to private or individual property, absurd and irrational systems of religion, and marriage."

ROBERT OWEN,
"A DECLARATION OF
MENTAL INDEPENDENCE"

JULY 4, 1826, was a momentous day. Exactly fifty years had passed since the Declaration of Independence had been signed. The United States was a half century old.

On that same day, within the space of a few hours, two of the most famous signers of the Declaration died: Thomas Jefferson and John Adams.

In his last letter, Jefferson had noted that freedom to think and freedom to express one's thoughts were essential if man was to be truly free. With his well-known concern for the future of his country, he added the thought that slaves could not be expected to put up with slavery forever.

"The mass of mankind," he wrote, "has not been born with saddles on their backs, nor a favored few booted and spurred, ready to ride them legitimately, by the grace of God."

When he heard the news, Lafayette wrote from La Grange to his old friend Madison: "Our beloved Jefferson is no more . . . . My dear friend, we are few remaining from old revolutionary times . . . ."

He added a note about Nashoba: "I have had letters from my beloved friends Fanny and Camilla Wright. They are . . . furthering their philanthropic experiment. . . . They deserve to be encouraged."

Word of the deaths did not reach New Harmony immediately. On that Tuesday in July while the two former Presidents lay dying, the mood of New Harmony was happy and optimistic. The little band of radicals and reformers was celebrating the great day. They trooped into the hall to hear Robert Owen, Dale's father, deliver the Fourth of July oration. He called it "A Declaration of Mental Independence."

The American Revolution of 1776, said Owen, was a political victory. It took power from the king and Parliament and gave it to the ordinary people. As a result, in all the world only Americans had the power to think freely and to express their opinions openly.

"Yes, my friends," he said, "the Declaration of Independence, in 1776, prepared the way to secure to you mental liberty. . . . The right of mental liberty is inherent in our nature . . . but until the Revolution of 1776, no people had acquired the political power to permit them to use that right . . . . This right, this invaluable right, you now enjoy by the Constitution."

Now that the American people had the right to think and speak freely, they must start a second revolution, said Owen. A revolution against three "monstrous evils." He listed these evils as private property, religion, and marriage. "This three-fold horrid monster is the real and only cause of all the crime, and misery arising from crime, which can be found in human society."

Owen went on to explain his views.

Private property, he said, meant that some people would be rich while most people would be poor. In order to abolish poverty, all wealth should be owned in common.

Religion, he went on, is nothing but superstition. It keeps men from thinking clearly. It forces them to believe in a God who is supposed to be kind, all-powerful, and wise. And yet one can see that the world is filled with violence, war, and bloodshed. Thus men are compelled to believe in something which is obviously false; they are made irrational. Religion, he concluded, "has caused more than its third of the crimes and sufferings of the human race."

Finally, Owen objected to requiring men and women to marry in order to be allowed to love one another. Marriage, added Owen, makes women slaves of their husbands.

But to be successful, said Owen, marriage must take place between equals. Since women did not have equality, forcing them into marriage in order to be supported

—there were almost no occupations open to women— was like forcing them into slavery. Girls were brought up, he charged, to trade their happiness and personal freedom for the economic security of marriage.

Owen concluded that a second revolution against private property, religion, and marriage would make man truly free. This revolution was necessary, he said, in order "that the many may be no longer poor wretched beings, dependent on the wealthy and powerful few; that Man may be no longer a superstitious idiot, continually dying from the futile fear of death; that he may no longer unite himself to the other sex from any mercenary or superstitious motives . . ."

To Fanny, much of Owen's "Declaration of Mental Independence" sounded familiar. She had long held similar ideas about wealth, about religion, and about marriage. But he had planted a new seed with his insistence on the importance of mental liberty.

Could the world be changed for the better if people kept on thinking in the same old way? Could slavery be ended by a small experiment at Nashoba as long as masters still thought like masters and slaves still thought like slaves?

Did the world need a *revolution* in the way people lived in order to change their *thinking,* or did their *thinking* have to be changed before there could be a *revolution?*

Which came first?

Chapter 16 THE NASHOBA PLAN

"We agree perfectly with the opinion Frances Wright has expressed on this subject; let the white man educate his children to be independent of the labor of slavery, while the young Negro is trained to profit by the gift of liberty."

BENJAMIN LUNDY

It was possible to talk philosophy and write pamphlets without knowing how to farm.

George Flower knew how to farm. But he was preoccupied with his own family. His children fell sick, one after the other. One day he packed them up and took them all back to Albion. He never returned.

Perhaps he was torn between love for Fanny and love for his wife. There is no proof that they were lovers at Nashoba. Yet Frances Trollope told the Garnett sisters that Fanny and George had lived together as man and wife while they were at the farm.

James Richardson hated slavery, opposed marriage, believed in freedom between the sexes, and was a good bookkeeper. But he knew nothing about farming.

Richesson Whitby had followed Camilla back to Nashoba when the Wright girls returned there from New Harmony in the late spring of 1826. He took George Flower's place and tried to see to it that the work was done and done properly. But he was too gentle and weak-willed to be a boss. His mind was on Camilla, when it should have been on plowing, planting, and weeding.

Dale had not followed Fanny back to Nashoba. He was no farmer, either. But perhaps his presence there would have been of help.

There were thirty blacks, half of them men and half women. They represented a sizeable investment of Fanny's fortune, a total of $6,000. On them rested the success of Nashoba.

They did not pay much mind to Fanny's lectures. It was pleasant to be told they were working for their freedom; but they really could not believe it. The land was her property, and so were they. *Freedom* was just a word in white people's mouths.

It made no difference how hard or how well they worked. No one beat them. They were fed whether they worked well or not. And so they worked the way slaves always work: grudgingly when forced to, carelessly when left alone.

Perhaps they heard something about the condition of their black brothers and sisters. In the cities there were free blacks. In New York slavery would be illegal in a few months. There was a large and important free black community in New York City.

Frances Wright. *(Courtesy of Miriam Holden)*

The Park Theater, where *Altorf* was performed in 1819. *(New York Public Library Picture Collection)*

New York City as it looked when Fanny and Camilla arrived on the *Amity* in 1818. *(New York Public Library Picture Collection)*

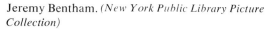

Jeremy Bentham. *(New York Public Library Picture Collection)*

Lafayette at the tomb of Washington. *(The Bettmann Archive, Inc.)*

Lafayette's arrival in New York. *(New York Public Library Picture Collection)*

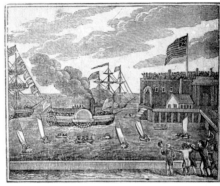

Henry Inman's portrait of Frances Wright, painted in 1824. *(Courtesy of The New-York Historical Society, New York City)*

A BIRD'S EYE VIEW OF ONE OF THE **NEW COMMUNITIES** AT **HARMONY**.
IN THE STATE OF INDIANA NORTH AMERICA.
AN ASSOCIATION OF TWO THOUSAND PERSONS FORMED UPON THE PRINCIPLES ADVOCATED BY
ROBERT OWEN
STEDMAN WHITWELL. ARCHITECT

The commune at New Harmony. *(Courtesy of The New-York Historical Society, New York City)*

Robert Dale Owen as an old man.
(New York Public Library Picture Collection)

Mrs. Trollope. *(New York Public Library Picture Collection)*

Cincinnati, the "Queen City of the West," in the early nineteenth century. *(New York Public Library Picture Collection)*

Auguste Hervieu's sketch of Nashoba, made in 1827. (*From* Domestic Manners of the Americans *by Frances Trollope, Edited by Donald Smalley*)

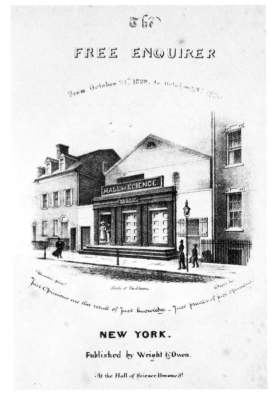

The Hall of Science, Broome Street, New York City. (*Courtesy of The New-York Historical Society, New York City*)

THE RIKER ESTATE FOOT OF 75th ST. EAST RIVER.

The Riker Estate, where the free enquirers lived in 1829. *(Courtesy of The New-York Historical Society, New York City)*

Richard M. Johnson, portrayed on the flyleaf of a volume of the *Free Enquirer. (Courtesy of Miriam Holden)*

The New York City
Debtors' Prison. *(New York
Public Library Picture
Collection)*

A DOWNRIGHT GABBLER,
or a goose that deserves to be hissed—

A contemporary caricature of Fanny Wright as a lecturing goose.
(Courtesy of The New-York Historical Society, New York City)

It had its own schools and theater. In the theater, the African Grove, white people were expected to sit in the back because "whites do not know how to conduct themselves at entertainments for ladies and gentlemen of color."

Blacks often ran away from slavery. On occasion they fought bloody battles for their freedom. The Nashoba blacks may have heard of all these happenings. There is no evidence that other blacks ever heard of Nashoba.

In addition to the incompetence of the whites and the indifference of the blacks, there was the weather. In the winter Nashoba was a prison of ice and snow. The settlers froze in the poorly constructed cabins. In the spring the rains turned the earth into a sea of thick mud and soupy clay. Clouds of mosquitoes stung and bit them. When the sun came out, vapor steamed from their sodden clothes. In the cabins the air was damp and musty.

The mosquitoes brought malaria and dengue in the summer of 1826. The settlers grew sick and listless. Fanny's bones ached; her teeth chattered with fever. She lay for days, alternately sweating and freezing. Camilla tried to nurse her. Richardson put his meager medical knowledge to work. Alone with the slaves, Richesson Whitby struggled to get the work done.

When Fanny felt better, she got up and worked. In the hot summer sun she cut brush and dug trenches. She rode all day through the woods, searching for lost cattle.

Nothing in her childhood had prepared her for such a life. By the end of August she was sick again. In addition to fever she suffered from sunstroke. She lay delirious for days. Richardson was worried. Camilla was frightened.

The work of the farm faltered. August passed into September. It looked as if the crop would barely pay for the food and supplies they would need to buy in Memphis. Fanny would have to dip into her own money once again.

Worried by her own illness, Fanny decided in the fall of 1826 to change the legal structure of Nashoba. It was foolish to keep it a one-woman charity project with everything in her name. If she were to die, the blacks might be sold into slavery. Someone might seize control of Nashoba for his own profit. The commune needed more money and more people. It needed wider support.

Fanny drew up a deed, a legal document describing the ownership of a particular piece of land. In her deed to Nashoba she shared ownership of the property with ten other trustees. She was the eleventh. The ten were Lafayette, Robert Owen, Robert Dale Owen, James Richardson, Robert Jennings, George Flower, Camilla, Richesson Whitby, William Maclure, and Cadwallader Colden. These eleven trustees would be Nashoba's governing body.

Maclure was a rich reformer interested in education. She had met him at New Harmony. He was a partner of Robert Owen's and had provided the funds for the experimental school there. He had brought William Phiquepal D'Arusmont over from France to run the school.

Colden was a former mayor of New York and a good friend of Charles Wilkes's, Fanny's old friend there. Although he was a conservative, he had been in the Park Theater the night *Altorf* was produced.

Colden had no idea Fanny was using his name, nor had any of the trustees. But the others were all radicals and agreed with her views. Colden did not.

Her deed to Nashoba listed the rules and regulations of the community. The hard work would be done by the blacks, working their way to freedom. The whites would provide supervision. But "no life of idleness is proposed to the whites," she wrote. "Those who cannot work must give an equivalent in property."

Thus right at the outset her experiment was flawed by the same inequality that she saw more clearly when she examined American slavery: the blacks would do the work; the whites would be the rulers. A white could become a member of Nashoba without working if he could provide $200 a year, which limited the white membership to wealthy people. To the blacks Nashoba must have looked exactly like a slave plantation, despite Fanny's intentions.

She insisted that there be a school for Nashoba's children and that it be racially integrated. "No difference will be made in the schools between the white children, and the children of color, whether in education or any other advantage."

The deed expressed Fanny's fears that freed blacks could never be safe in the United States. At the very outset it provided that "all Negroes emancipated by the trustees, shall on quitting the lands of the institution, be placed out of the limits of the United States."

She set up her own board of trustees, because she distrusted both the colonization societies and the emancipation (later abolition) societies. "The colonization societies," she said bluntly, are "favorable to slavery."

She respected the emancipation societies but could not accept their religious outlook. She described them as "real friends of the liberty of man." But she rejected their moralizing. Later she would oppose the abolitionists for their insistence that slavery was a moral issue, and for their religious and political conservatism.

To Fanny organized religion was mental slavery. She had felt that way as a young girl, and now the ideas of Robert Owen reinforced that feeling.

Another reason she named the trustees was to attract attention and support. Names like Owen and Lafayette and Maclure were known and respected all over the world. Perhaps she included a conservative like Colden as "window dressing."

Despite the trustees, Fanny was very much in charge. There was no one else with her will, intelligence, and dedication. Except for Camilla and Whitby, and Richardson, and occasionally Robert Dale Owen, none of the trustees ever set foot on the land of Nashoba.

The spirit of the community was to be the spirit of persuasion. "We must come to the slaveholder not in anger but in kindness," Fanny wrote, "and when we ask him to change his whole mode of life we must show him the means by which he may do so." She hoped that slaveholders would voluntarily come to Nashoba with their families and their slaves. If not, she hoped they would at least send the children of their slaves to be trained for freedom, and their own children to be raised so that they should not feel they must be masters.

The deed also invited white people who were not slaveholders. "Those who have money or other property will bring it; those who have only their arms or their heads will bring them."

Everything was to be accomplished by education. The principal object, she said, "is the improvement of the slave, and the fitting him for the condition of a free man, by cultivating in him good feelings and inspiring him with habits of care and economy."

She did not fool herself that many whites would want or even be able to afford membership in her commune. But she was convinced that Nashoba offered advantages to people who thought the way she and Dale and the others at New Harmony thought.

"In this conviction," she wrote to a friend, "I have devoted my time and fortune to laying the foundations of an establishment where affection shall form the only marriage, kind feeling and kind action the only religion, respect for the feelings of others the only restraint. . . ."

Benjamin Lundy approved of her plan. He published the deed to Nashoba in his *Genius of Universal Emancipation*, adding the following editorial note: "We perfectly agree with the opinion Frances Wright has expressed on this subject; let the white man educate his children to be independent of the labor of slavery, while the young Negro is trained to profit by the gift of liberty."

Fanny's views on marriage are reflected in one regulation concerning the admission of new members. "The admission of a husband will not carry along with it as a consequence the admission of his wife . . . . Nor the admission of a wife the admission of her husband." Thus each individual was to be admitted to Nashoba on his or her own merits by a unanimous vote of the trustees in residence. "Perfect independence," wrote Fanny, "is one of the objects of this deed."

Exhausted by a summer of hard work and fever, and by her efforts at reorganizing her commune, Fanny left Nashoba in early winter and rode back to New Harmony once more. She took with her in her saddlebag a copy of the deed. Perhaps she could find more recruits for the struggling little experiment on the Wolf River.

She would have liked Robert Jennings to come and set up a school. But he had left New Harmony and gone back east to his family. He was working as a reporter for a liberal newspaper in New York.

She really wanted Robert Dale Owen.

Dale was bored and restless. New Harmony was ending its cooperative experiment. Its farmers were now renting their land from his father. Fanny's second appearance in his life must have seemed a lucky accident.

He was overcome with pride when he learned that she had made him a trustee. It was quite an honor for a young man in his twenties. It was especially gratifying to have his name associated with such famous personages as Lafayette, Maclure, and his own father.

Fanny stayed at New Harmony for the winter, trying to regain her health and strength. She and Dale became very close. In the spring of 1827 the two went back to Tennessee together.

On the way her illness returned. By the time they reached Memphis, she was so weak she could no longer ride her horse. Dale found a wagon and driver, and the two men slung a hammock for her. On the thirteen-mile trip from Memphis to Nashoba, Fanny lay half asleep in the lurching hammock, too weak even to sit up.

At Nashoba Dale found only three other trustees present: Whitby, Richardson, and Camilla. He was disappointed at the signs of failure all around, in contrast to what Fanny's bubbling enthusiasm had led him to expect.

The land was obviously second-rate. Of the two thousand acres only a hundred had been cleared of trees. The only buildings that had been erected were four crude log cabins and a handful of wretched shanties in which the slaves lived.

The slaves were not working very hard. No one seemed to know what to do. Richesson Whitby was poorly organized and unsure of himself.

Richardson took one look at Fanny and told her she ought to leave Tennessee before the hot weather returned. He described her illness of the past summer to Dale, and urged a long rest.

Fanny was of two minds. She hated to admit her physical weakness. But on the other hand it was clear she would have to do something to find more members for Nashoba. Planters were not rushing to bring either their slaves or their sons. Perhaps she might find some new allies among her old friends in France and England.

When Richardson suggested a sea voyage and a vacation in Europe, she agreed. She told Dale, with her customary sparkle, that there were sure to be liberals in Paris and London who would flock to Nashoba. She asked him to go with her. Dale, casting a dubious look around the dreary clearing in the woods of Tennessee, was delighted to get away.

Richesson Whitby objected that the slaves would not obey him if both Fanny and Camilla left. He insisted that Camilla stay. "You are their owner and mistress," he told Fanny. "They will not listen to me if I do not have one of you here to back me up." Camilla agreed to remain.

Before they left Nashoba for Memphis and the steamboat that would take them down the Mississippi River to New Orleans, Dale had a chance to see some of the nightly meetings between the trustees and the slaves. Minutes of these meetings were recorded by Richardson in the daily journal of Nashoba.

On the evening of May 7, the journal reports, "Frances Wright endeavored to explain to them [the slaves] the powers with which she had invested the trustees, her reason for investing them with this power, and the resolutions which the trustees passed."

The journal entry for May 7 also tells something about the daily life of the slaves and their problems:

"Dilly and Redick were reprimanded for interchanging abusive language, instead of laying their respective complaints before us.

"Willis was made to retract the threat which he had uttered of avenging with his own hands the wrongs of Dilly.

"Kitty was reprimanded for washing and receiving pay for washing the clothes of Mr. Roe, instead of carrying them to Sukey, the washerwoman. She was also made to return the twenty-five cents to Mr. R."

One week later, Fanny and Dale left for Europe. In New Orleans, while waiting for their ship, Fanny visited certain people in the free black community there.

She had now concluded that free blacks were the key to the success of Nashoba. They would have to be involved in her project if it was to flourish. She did not say too much about this, because she knew that most white Americans, including her prominent supporters, hated and feared the idea of free blacks living among whites.

In New Orleans the free blacks she spoke to were intensely interested in her commune. One of them told her, "I cannot be happy until I see Nashoba."

Fanny hired a free black woman to be the schoolteacher at Nashoba. Mlle. Lolotte, the daughter of a black mother and a white father, was herself the mother of a number of children born of a white father. Her teen-age daughter, Josephine, was extremely beautiful. Josephine went to Nashoba with her mother, but since she was over fourteen years of age, by the rules of the deed she had to be accepted by the trustees on her own personal merits and not just as her mother's daughter. She therefore became a probationary member of the community.

A few days after she saw Mlle. Lolotte with her young children and Josephine safely aboard the riverboat to Memphis, Fanny sailed with Dale for France.

During her absence in Europe, Nashoba's troubles grew. James Richardson fell in love with Josephine and proceeded to live with her as man and wife. He noted this fact carefully in the Nashoba journal, and insisted on announcing it to the world. He considered it entirely proper for an unmarried man and woman to live together so long as neither was forced by the other to do so. As to the matter of Josephine's race, he was totally unconcerned.

Nashoba was then attacked in the press as a place of sexual immorality. The attacks were stimulated by Richardson's refusal to recognize racial distinctions. Camilla defended both Richardson and Nashoba. She added that both she and Fanny approved of free love without marriage.

Despite her gentleness and her shyness, Camilla could, on occasion, be as strong and sturdy as her older sister. She could sometimes be even more forthright because she was not concerned, as Fanny was, with putting her philosophy in the best possible public light.

When Charles Wilkes, their conservative old banker friend in New York, wrote asking for an explanation, Camilla expressed her "entire disapproval of the marriage tie." She described marriage as "irrational" and "pernicious." She called it "one of the most subtle inventions of priestcraft for poisoning the purest source of human felicity."

Camilla defended Richardson and announced that her sister's "views of the sexual relation" were the same as her own. To make sure that the world did not miss the point, she sent copies of her letter to friends in Europe, asking them to tell Lafayette exactly how she and Fanny felt about marriage. And she instructed Wilkes to do the same for their American friends.

Ever since slavery began, white masters had been taking sexual advantage of their female slaves. They often fathered children in this way. Sex without marriage between white and black was nothing new.

What *was* new was the fact that James Richardson had openly announced his relationship with Josephine and lived with her publicly. He treated her as his wife. In fact, she was free and not a slave. Camilla supported them fully.

Chapter 17 WHAT MRS. TROLLOPE SAW

"It must have been some [powerful] feeling . . . which enabled Miss Wright, accustomed to all the comfort and refinement of Europe, to imagine not only that she herself could exist in this wilderness, but that her European friends could enter there, and not feel discouraged at the savage aspect of the scene."

FRANCES TROLLOPE

FANNY and Dale had a delightful ocean voyage. Her health improved with each day that took her farther from America. By July, when their ship reached port at Le Havre, she was almost her old self again.

The two spent several weeks together in Paris. Fanny went to see Lafayette, and took her young man along to meet the famous old general.

Lafayette was his usual generous self. He invited Dale to spend a weekend at his place, La Grange, and offered to pick him up in his carriage. Dale was ecstatic. "I was at the summit of human felicity," he wrote. Imagine, he added, "the privilege of a talk in uninterrupted quiet during a four or five hour drive, with a leading spirit in two revolutions!" While Dale worshiped at Lafayette's feet, Fanny was busy visiting old friends and trying to drum up recruits for Nashoba.

In August Dale went to Scotland to visit his mother, and then to England to see what support he could find among English radicals. He took with him a long letter from Fanny to Mary Shelley, widow of the poet Percy Shelley.

Mary Shelley, just two years younger than Fanny, was the daughter of Mary Wollstonecraft. Her mother had died at her birth, and she had been raised by her father, the radical philosopher William Godwin. Shelley had died in 1822, leaving her with a young son. She was attractive, intelligent, quite radical in her views, and the author of many books. Her most famous work was the novel *Frankenstein,* written when she was scarcely twenty-one years old. Fanny was burning to meet the daughter of the first woman to put forth the idea of women's liberation.

In her letter Fanny described Nashoba and its principles. She mentioned her difficulties there. She hinted that she would like to meet Mary. "If you possess the opinions of your father, and the generous feelings of your mother, I feel that I could travel far to see you." She added, "I wish to convey to Mary Wollstonecraft Godwin Shelley my respect and admiration of those from whom she holds those names." Mail would reach her in Paris, she concluded, "in care of General Lafayette."

Dale found Mary Shelley as attractive as Fanny. In

his later years he regretted that he had not met her first. He thought she might have been better for him. She was gentler and less radical. But at that time of his life, still in his twenties, he may have needed a strong, dominant woman like Fanny.

Mary wrote back inviting Fanny to come to Brighton to visit her. Fanny was overjoyed. She would have liked Mary to join her at Nashoba. Soon, she wrote, "I run back to my forests . . . . I want one of my own sex to commune with, and sometimes to lean upon in all the confidence of equality of friendship." Perhaps she felt that only individuals of the same sex could have a relationship based on equality.

The two young women did not have much of a visit in England: Fanny came to London but was unable to go to Brighton. Mary and her son had to stay in Brighton. On November 4, 1827, just as Fanny's ship was about to sail from London for America, the women met briefly on the dock. Then they watched each other disappearing into the distance as the water widened between the ship and the port. Dale was to sail from Liverpool in January.

Fanny had not been successful in finding recruits for Nashoba. On board the *Edward* with her was her old friend Frances Trollope, with her teen-age son and two little daughters, two servants, and a young French artist who lived with the Trollopes.

Frances Trollope's husband, Thomas, had been very helpful seven years earlier in finding a publisher for Fanny's first book, *Views of Society and Manners in*

America. When the Trollopes visited France in 1824, Fanny returned the favor and made their trip a social success by introducing them to Lafayette. Since then, she and the Trollopes had become great friends. The Trollopes by no means shared Fanny's opinions on religion, marriage, and politics. They were quite conventional upper-class people. But Frances Trollope was a lively sociable person, and she enjoyed the company of revolutionists and radicals as long as they were well educated and charming. She found them exciting company.

Fanny had spent some time with the Trollopes during the weeks in England when she could not see Mary Shelley. She could not have arrived, from the Trollopes' point of view, at a better time.

The Trollope family—there were five children; one of them, Anthony, later became the famous writer—had fallen on hard times. Mr. Trollope's law practice had been going downhill for some years. Now they were almost bankrupt, finding it hard to make ends meet. They tried desperately to keep up their big house, and pay their servants' wages, but they were going further into debt each day.

Fanny seemed to offer Frances Trollope a way out of these difficulties. What she said about the efforts at Nashoba to educate and free blacks did not concern the Trollopes very much. But the thought of spending some time there as Fanny's guest sounded both interesting and attractive to Frances.

What was most important to Mr. Trollope was the

idea of making a lot of money in America. Many Europeans, especially Englishmen, were thinking up schemes
to make their fortunes in the New World. In England,
that summer, the city of Cincinnati had been getting a
good deal of publicity as the thriving metropolis of the
American West.

A busy river port of twenty thousand inhabitants on
the edge of the backwoods, it was the largest city in the
Mississippi Valley. The bulk of European trade with the
American West came by sailing ship to New Orleans
and then up the Mississippi River by steamboat to Cincinnati.

Mr. Trollope had the idea of setting up a store there
to sell fancy goods from London and Paris to the American settlers. He was sure the store would be a great success and make the family fortune.

Nashoba was south and west of Cincinnati. Mrs.
Trollope, with three of her children and two servants,
would go there to stay with Fanny Wright for a few
months. At her leisure she would then proceed to Cincinnati to look it over and make plans for the great ven-
ture. Mr. Trollope would stay in England to raise
money and buy stock for the store. In a year he would
join his family.

Frances Trollope took almost no money with her. As
Fanny's guest she did not think she would need any.
With her, in addition to her children and servants, was
the French artist Auguste Hervieu. This young man was
a political refugee from reactionary France. He was a

family friend of the Trollopes, and at their house he had heard Fanny talk glowingly of Nashoba and of the school she had established. He had decided to come along to teach art there.

On Christmas Day 1827, the *Edward* reached the mouth of the Mississippi. Two days later it docked at New Orleans, and Fanny and her party disembarked to wait for a steamboat to take them up the river to Memphis.

Frances Trollope was not favorably impressed with what she saw. She described her impressions in a travel book quite different in tone from Fanny's earlier book. To Mrs. Trollope, America was not the promised land, and Americans were not a new and better type of humanity. In keeping with her conservative political views she did not have much sympathy for the young democratic republic.

In her book, *Domestic Manners of the Americans,* she drew a critical picture of the social customs and the daily behavior she observed. She looked with a sharp eye, and wrote with a sharper pen.

"I hardly knew any annoyance so deeply repugnant to English feelings," Frances Trollope said, "as the incessant, remorseless spitting of Americans . . . . The gentlemen in the cabin [of the steamboat] would certainly neither, from their language, manners, nor appearance have received that designation in Europe . . . ."

Their steamboat reached Memphis at midnight in the
midst of a heavy rainstorm. They made their way to the
hotel there through thick mud.

Despite the mud, they set off the next day for
Nashoba, traveling in a wagon drawn by a team of
horses. They seemed to be traveling through a dark
leafy tunnel. The trees were so thick and close they
could see neither sun nor sky.

The driver took the wagon down a riverbank and out
into the water in order to avoid crossing on a shaky log
bridge. Soon the water was up over the hubs of the
wheels; then it reached the floorboards of the wagon.
The horses began to lose their footing. The river ahead
was even deeper.

The driver stopped and turned to face his passengers.
"I expect we'll have to unhitch the horses and ride back
on them," he said pleasantly. "We're in a fix here."

Fanny sat composed and smiling. "Yes, Jacob," she
said. "That is what we must do." And so the Trollopes,
Hervieu, and Fanny had to mount the horses from the
stalled wagon and ride back to Memphis on them.
Fanny was cheerful and lighthearted through it all.

It occurred to Mrs. Trollope that the closer they came
to Nashoba the more changed Fanny Wright seemed.

The next day Fanny left her friends and rode on
alone through the mud to Nashoba. The day after that,
the Trollopes and Auguste Hervieu set out again, this
time in a Dearborn, a high-wheeled carriage. Finally,
after some hours, they arrived at the settlement.

"One glance," wrote Mrs. Trollope, "sufficed to convince me that every idea I had formed of the place was as far as possible from the truth." The word that sprang to her mind to describe Nashoba was desolation.

She looked around and saw a small clearing surrounded by trees and swamps. There were a half-dozen crude log cabins. A group of listless black slaves, Mlle. Lalotte and her small children, and three bedraggled white people—Fanny, Richesson Whitby, and Camilla —were the only human beings at the settlement. James Richardson and Josephine had eloped a month earlier.

When Frances Trollope had last seen Camilla, she had been a lively, pretty young woman. Now she seemed much older and thinner, pale and feverish from malaria.

Auguste Hervieu looked for his art studio. "Where is the school?" he asked Fanny. When she told him that it had not yet been built, he swore with rage. He insisted he would return to Memphis as soon as he could.

Frances Trollope began to worry about her children. There was no milk at Nashoba. All they had to drink was rain water. There was a little wheat bread, but the bulk of the bread was made from Indian corn and was inedible to the Trollopes. There was no fruit, no vegetables, only rice. There was no meat but pork—no butter, no cheese, no eggs.

Fanny, Mrs. Trollope observed, seemed oblivious to the hardships. "To do her justice," she wrote, "I believe her mind was so exclusively occupied by the object that she had then in view, that all things else were worthless or indifferent to her."

Despite her intense disappointment, Frances Trollope maintained a balanced view of Fanny. She could see that her old friend was in the grip of a passionate idea. "The Frances Wright of Nashoba, in dress, looks, and manner, bore no more resemblance to the Miss Wright I had known and admired in London and Paris than did her log cabin to the Tuileries or Buckingham Palace."

She saw that Fanny shared the same hardships as everyone else and that she did so with good spirit. "I shared her bedroom," she said. "It had no ceiling, and the floor consisted of planks laid loosely on piles, that raised it some feet from the earth. The rain had access through the wooden roof, and the chimney, which was of logs slightly plastered with mud, caught fire at least a dozen times a day; but Frances Wright stood in the midst of all this desolation, with the air of a conqueror; she would say, perhaps, that she was so, since she had triumphed over all human weakness."

Auguste Hervieu left Nashoba almost immediately. Frances Trollope stayed on for a while. But she continued to worry about her children's health. When she asked Camilla about her illness, Camilla told her it was a result of the climate. She described dengue and malaria, and the chills and fever they brought. Thoroughly frightened, Mrs. Trollope decided to follow Hervieu to Memphis.

But she had no money. And so on January 23 the three trustees at Nashoba—Fanny, Camilla, and

Whitby—lent her three hundred dollars. A few days later the Trollopes left.

Frances Trollope and Fanny Wright would meet again. The former respected her friend's idealism even though she did not share it. "Her whole heart and soul," she wrote years later, "were occupied by the hope of raising the African . . . . Even now I cannot recall the self-devotion with which she gave herself to it without admiration."

Chapter 18 **END OF**
A DREAM

"Collective humanity is alone able to
effect what I . . . thought myself
equal to attempt alone."

FRANCES WRIGHT

EVEN before she sailed from London with the Trollopes,
Fanny had known that Nashoba was in serious difficulties. Richardson's love affair with Josephine and his
defiance of white supremacy customs had become a
public scandal.

Fanny had written to Richardson from La Grange
when she heard the rumors. She did not disapprove of
his relationship with Josephine. She did not disagree
with his boldly expressed opinions on marriage and
race. They were her opinions, too.

But she thought it wiser to keep such views private in
order not to antagonize the public. Nashoba needed all
the help it could get. It would be a pity, she said, if they
were to be defeated because of personal behavior or
opinions that had nothing at all to do with ending slavery—and ending slavery was her main goal. "All princi-

ples are liable to misinterpretation," she wrote, "but none so much as ours." Although she agreed with Camilla, Fanny would not have been as outspoken as her sister. But she kept her criticism to herself. She knew that a harsh word from her would hurt Camilla terribly.

In order to meet criticism, and in order to win even wider public support, Fanny wrote a brief description of the philosophy underlying Nashoba and sent it to all her friends and every newspaper she could think of. This document—*Explanatory Notes, respecting the nature and object of the institution at Nashoba*—caused more trouble than anything Richardson or Camilla did or said. In it she set forth quite frankly her opinions on marriage, sex, religion, and race.

What was most shocking to Americans was her belief that for the good of the country the black and white races ought to blend together. Future generations, she implied, would intermarry—the word she used was amalgamate—and in time all Americans would be one color. She looked forward to a future America in which "the means shall be sought, and found, and employed to develop all the intellectual and physical powers of all human beings, without regard to sex or condition—class, race, or color."

She said she hoped for an America and a world in which all people were in fact "members of one great family, with equal claims to enjoyment and equal capacities for labor and instruction . . . ." It was the aim of Nashoba, she added, to show by example that such a happy result was possible.

These ideas were too much even for those who had
been her supporters. James Madison complained to Lafayette: "Her views of amalgamating the white and
black population [are] universally obnoxious." He also
objected to "her notions on the spirit of religion and of
marriage."

Friends had written to her while she was still in Europe that throughout the South people had been heard
to say that they would "not be surprised if Miss Wright
should, one of these mornings, find her throat cut."

Liberal newspapers were somewhat more favorable to
her views. But they commented pointedly on her brav-
ery in voicing them. The New York *Correspondent*
thought her ideas ought to be confined to one small
community.

When she had reached Nashoba one day ahead of the
Trollopes, Fanny had learned that Richardson and Josephine had run off together, and that Camilla and
Richesson Whitby had married, despite Camilla's opposition to marriage. According to the Nashoba journal
they were married by a justice of the peace while Fanny
and the Trollopes were still at sea. The journal entry, in
Camilla's handwriting, added that she still considered
the marriage tie "irrational" but that she did not wish to
antagonize public opinion.

After saying good-bye to the Trollopes, Fanny added
up the records for the year 1827 and found that
Nashoba had produced seventy-five pounds of corn,
eight dozen eggs, sixty-eight pounds of butter, seventy-
three chickens, and barely sixty dollars' worth of cotton.

Instead of earning a part of their freedom by paying back Fanny for their purchase, the slaves now actually owed money to the commune.

Fanny decided to cancel the accounts for the year. She wanted the slaves to show a credit toward their emancipation. But to continue she would have to keep pouring her own money into Nashoba. Financially her experiment in freedom through collective living was a failure.

Dale returned from England. He, too, had not brought a single recruit. Camilla and Richesson grew sicker. Finally Fanny had to hire a professional overseer to run the farm. At the end of February Camilla and Richesson returned once more to New Harmony.

At almost the same time a letter arrived from Robert Jennings in New York. He had fallen on hard times, and he wanted to bring his family to Nashoba. It was clear from the letter that he was looking for a comfortable place where he would not have to work to earn a living.

Fanny did not mislead him. "My dear Jennings," she wrote, "co-operation has well nigh killed us all . . . . You cannot hold the plough, plant corn or sow cabbages. If you try . . . it will put you out of the world."

She advised him to stay in New York and work for their political goals there. "Exert yourself for the time being in forwarding the cause of liberal principles in the East . . . ."

Fanny still believed in Nashoba, and still believed in collective living. But she had decided that only a new and younger generation could bring such principles about. Youth would first have to be trained in how to live and how to work in a society that was not competitive.

Despite her frequent illness, her lack of success, the failure of her friends to live up to her beliefs, and the loss of about sixteen thousand dollars—half her fortune—Fanny remained cheerful and optimistic. To Jennings she wrote that she was "firmer in my purpose, more inflexible in principle, [but] enriched with experience." But the older generation—her generation—seemed to be a lost cause.

Fanny was lonelier now, with Camilla away. Although she had never met Dale's mother, Mary Owen, she wrote to her in Scotland. She excused herself for writing directly on the grounds of her "affectionate intimacy" with Dale.

Mary Owen would never have guessed, from this letter, that the experiment at Nashoba had almost ended. Fanny assured her that life in Nashoba offered advantages to Dale. "We are now but a small circle," she wrote, "and are not likely ever to embrace a very large one, drawn as our companions must be from the morally cultivated and also from those possessed of small but independent incomes. Yet if I judge correctly Robert's tastes and character it is in a society composed of such elements that he may best receive and impart happiness and select, with best opportunity for selecting well, a suitable companion of the other sex."

She assured Mrs. Owen that her son was "with those who love him dearly and value him highly."

But Dale was not cut out for the rugged life of Nashoba. When his father came by on a short visit, he went with him to New Harmony to put the *New Harmony Gazette* back on its feet. In the absence of Dale and Jennings the paper had begun to deteriorate. And New Harmony was losing money.

Mlle. Lolotte left with her children to join her daughter Josephine, now Mrs. James Richardson. Fanny was now practically alone at Nashoba. She lived quietly in her cabin, writing, reading, and thinking. The slaves worked under the overseer in another part of the plantation.

She wrote to friends. To Mary Shelley she wrote bravely: "Dear Mary, I do find the quiet of these forests and our ill-fenced cabins of rough logs now soothing to the spirit, and now no less suited to the body, than the warm luxurious houses of European society . . . to me the sacrifices are nothing."

Of Dale's short stay at Nashoba, she wrote: "Dale arrived, his sweet kind heart all unthawed, and truly when he left us for Harmony I think the very last thin flake of Scotch ice had melted from him."

One day a man named Otto Braun, a friend of Jeremy Bentham's, turned up at her cabin. He had walked all the way from Memphis just to see her and to have a look at her famous little commune. He talked with her for a while. He tried to convince her that Nashoba was a mistake and that she should abandon her wilderness experiment. But he failed. After a while he turned back through the forest.

After he reached Memphis, he sent her a long letter. In it he wrote: "You pretend to me that you are never going to marry. Good Miss Wright, you are already married to a soil which I will not call poor, but which I can compare to a big, swollen, heavy, lubberly, lazy, scurvy fellow . . . . He has cost you too much already in money and health."

He asked her to leave Nashoba and join him in Memphis. He offered her companionship. He urged her to come with him to New Harmony where he was going to talk with Robert Owen. "I shall wait for you, see you safe there, be your banker and steward on the road or river, and ask nothing in return."

He added a comment on her plans for building the perfect human society: "Frances Wright is evidently well endowed by nature. She has sense and talent and eloquence, but no chemical knowledge of the material, or geometric skill for the construction of any fabric suitable for an establishment of human happiness."

She did not answer his letter.

In late spring, just before the hot weather began, a long letter came from Dale. He called her "my sweet Fanny," and urged her to come to New Harmony. He needed her help in editing the *New Harmony Gazette*. Things looked bad. The paper was losing money. It needed a strong editor to take charge of it. As for New Harmony, there was now a dramatic society. It was anxious to produce liberal plays in the public hall there. Did she have half a dozen copies of *Altorf*? He added: "All your friends are anxious to see you."

Dale missed her. In England he had complained to Mary Shelley that Fanny did not pay much attention to him. Mary had sent him a note of sisterly advice.

"Take care of our Fanny, dear Dale," she had written, "she is neither so independent or so fearless as you think.

"Study to please Fanny—divine her uneasiness and be ever ready at her side with brotherly protection—do not imagine that she is capable always of taking care of herself . . . . she is too sensitive and feminine not largely to partake in this inherent part of us [women]—a desire to find a manly spirit whereon [to] lean—a manly arm to protect and shelter us . . . . The time perhaps is not far off when Fanny may find in a lover these necessities better supplied than you can supply them—but till then no man need be nearer—dearer or more useful to her than yourself—"

Fanny knew the dream of Nashoba was ending. But she did not consider it a total failure. She felt she had learned more during its two and a half years of existence than during any other period in her life. She had learned that individual experiments could not change the world. "Collective humanity is alone able to effect what I . . . thought myself equal to attempt alone."

Experiments like Nashoba could generate new ideas and teach lessons. But, she noted, "reform, to be effective, must be rightly understood in its principles by a collective body, and carried forward wisely and consistently, with due regard for the interests of all concerned."

Perhaps the *New Harmony Gazette* was the instrument to explain those principles.

A few days after Dale's letter the entry in the journal reads: "Frances Wright leaves Nashoba to join her sister at [New] Harmony, leaving the property in charge of John Gilliam."

V

To Change the World

Speak of "change" and the world is in alarm. And yet where do we not see change? What is there in the physical world but *change? . . . The flower blossoms, the fruit ripens, the seed is received and germinates in the earth, and we behold the tree. . . . All is change.*

—FRANCES WRIGHT, FOURTH OF JULY ORATION, 1828

Chapter 19 YEAR OF CHANGE

"It is not the legitimate province of the Legislature to determine what religion is true or what is false. Our government is a civil, and not a religious institution."
                                        SENATOR RICHARD M.
                                        JOHNSON, KENTUCKY

THE year 1828—the year Fanny quit Nashoba and moved to New Harmony—was a moody, restless year.

John Quincy Adams of Massachusetts was in the White House. Andrew Jackson of South Carolina and Tennessee ran against him for the Presidency. Jackson was the leader of the new Democratic party.

In the cities, growing numbers of mechanics, shop-keepers, and factory workers wanted a government that paid more attention to their problems. By 1828 many state laws limiting the vote to men with property had been changed. Poor and lower-middle class white men had now become voters. The ordinary white American was suddenly involved in politics.

Most of them voted for Jackson and his party. Jackson won the election of 1828, and his victory was cheered by poor white people all over the country. Blacks and Indians had no reason to feel happy. Nor did conservatives in New England and New York.

In the national capital President Adams sat in gloom. Chief Justice John Marshall worried about "the mob"— by which he meant the common people. Senator Daniel Webster wrote anxiously to friends: "General Jackson will be here about 15 February. Nobody knows what he will do when he does come . . . . My opinion is that he will bring a breeze with him. Which way it will blow I cannot tell . . . ."

In the year 1828, Fanny had more important things to worry about than politics. She and Dale and Robert Jennings and the other New Harmony radicals saw little difference between Jackson and Adams, but they were worried about the *New Harmony Gazette*. It had been losing readers and money steadily. New Harmony was in financial trouble and could not support it. The paper needed to find a wider audience.

The new political excitement stirred up by the election campaign encouraged them to look outside their own ranks for readers. People all over the country were open to new ideas. America's new problems had stimulated new demands, new reforms. A restless mood of change was sweeping the public.

Perhaps the New Harmony radicals ought to reach out to the people of the cities? Perhaps they should begin with nearby Cincinnati, which liked to call itself "Queen City of the West."

It was not an exaggeration. Cincinnati was the largest city in the West. Her churches, newspapers, and schools were outposts of civilization on the edge of the frontier.

Built on a lovely hill across the Ohio River from Kentucky, the town had some twenty thousand inhabitants, mostly Americans of Scottish, Irish, English, and German descent. There was a large minority of free blacks and a handful of Jews. The town grew and prospered on the rich river trade between the West and the rest of the country. It was, after all, only 450 miles by steamboat from Pittsburgh, 130 from Louisville, and 1,480 up the Mississippi from the great port of New Orleans. It had paper mills, glass factories, and iron foundries. A hog-slaughtering, pork-packing industry was just starting.

Cincinnati had a museum, three markets, and a theater. Junius Brutus Booth, the great Shakespearian actor just come over from England, was appearing there in *King Lear.*

Cincinnati also had churches—twenty-three of them. There were two Presbyterian churches, two Methodist, one Episcopal, one Baptist, one Swedenborgian, a Quaker meeting house, a Roman Catholic cathedral, and assorted houses of worship of Congregationalists, Mormons, Moravians, Shakers, and other Christian sects.

In 1828 Frances Trollope had arrived in Cincinnati with her children, in flight from the hardships of Nashoba. She stayed there for two years, trying to establish a department store as the Trollope family business. She was not successful.

But she did write an enormously successful book which earned her a lot of money. This book, *Domestic Manners of the Americans,* was an amusing, lively report to European readers of what life was like in the United

States. Mrs. Trollope did not see America, as Fanny did, through the eyes of a lover, but through the eyes of a critic.

In her book she describes Cincinnati in 1828 as "a city of extraordinary size and importance." She commented on its prosperity. Only thirty years before, she noted, the place on which the town now stood had been nothing but wild forest land.

But she also found Cincinnati dull and dreary. "I never saw any people who appeared to live so much without amusement as the Cincinnatians. Billiards are forbidden by law, so are cards. To sell a pack of cards in Ohio subjects the seller to a penalty of fifty dollars. They have no public balls excepting I think six during the Christmas holidays. They have no concerts. They have no dinner parties."

What struck her as especially disagreeable was the lack of social freedom for women. There was nothing they were allowed to do for their own enjoyment in public except go to church. The theater, which she found to be the only public amusement "in this sad little town," was off limits for ladies. It was considered un-Christian for a woman to be seen in a theater. In church, she noted, women dressed up in their best clothing and seemed to be enjoying some sort of recreation.

Although she was a conventional person in her beliefs and no enemy of religion, Mrs. Trollope had a poor opinion of American churches. She found the influence of the clergy over women much too strong and repressive. "I never saw or read of any country where religion had so strong a hold upon the women or a slighter hold upon the men." It almost seemed to her as if religion were a force that helped to keep women down. While she was in Cincinnati, she witnessed a scene that confirmed her dislike of religious practices there. She saw her first revival meeting.

The revival meeting held in Cincinnati in the summer of 1828 was part of a carefully planned national campaign. The churches of the East were alarmed at the free spirit and freethinking ways of the West. They had launched a great campaign for religious observance, and they asked for government support.

The church groups wanted federal laws passed forbidding travel on post roads on Sundays. They wanted laws forbidding the delivery of mail or the operation of any business on Sunday. They wanted all nonchurch activity on Sunday forbidden by law. In this way they hoped to force people back into the churches they had left of their own free will. They tried to organize a Christian party in politics to work for these laws.

These religious leaders were for the most part conservative eastern and New England ministers. They were strongly supported by the merchants, bankers, and factory owners. Many of these rich men were frightened at the new interest in politics shown by working people and mechanics. They were worried by the workers' demands to limit the hours of factory work from twelve and fifteen hours a day to only ten. These conservative leaders hoped to use religion as a political weapon against reform and change and the introduction of new ideas.

They were mostly National Republicans—supporters of John Quincy Adams in the presidential campaign of 1828. The rise of the Democratic party and its leader, Andrew Jackson, frightened them. Jackson's followers, and the general himself, believed in maintaining the separation of church and state enacted into law in the First Amendment to the Constitution.

The Democrats considered themselves the political descendants of Thomas Jefferson. Those old Jeffersonians still alive—James Madison, Albert Gallatin, DeWitt Clinton of New York—were strong believers in the separation of church and state and in religious liberty. Most of them were now Democrats. The more radical of Jackson's supporters took inspiration from the writings of Thomas Paine. Senator Richard M. Johnson of Kentucky was their political hero.

The revival meeting Frances Trollope witnessed was endorsed by many of the churches of Cincinnati. There were days of prayer meetings, sermon shouting, and hymn singing. Preachers worked up the crowds into moods of wild emotional excitement. People fell on their knees in the aisles and begged to be "saved."

Frances Trollope was disgusted by the hysteria she saw. "Young girls rose, and sat down, and rose again; and then the pews opened and several came tottering out, their hands clasped, their heads hanging on their

bosoms, and every limb trembling . . . as the poor creatures approached the rail their sobs and groans became
audible . . . increased to a frightful excess. Young creatures with features pale and distorted fell on their knees
on the pavement and soon sunk forward on their faces;
the most violent cries and shrieks followed . . . ."

She noted many such scenes of hysteria, and she saw
women in convulsions. She watched the clergymen whip
up the excitement to greater heights. "It was a frightful
sight to behold innocent young creatures, in the gay
morning of existence, thus seized upon, horror struck,
and rendered feeble and enervated forever." She saw
fourteen-year-old girls quivering, speaking in "tongues,"
and slavering at the mouth. She wondered what the men
of America must think of their wives and daughters to
allow such scenes.

Frances Trollope did not think there was much real
religious feeling in what she saw. "It is thus the ladies of
Cincinnati amuse themselves," she concluded tartly.

To Fanny Wright, a few hundred miles west down the
Ohio River at New Harmony, the revival was not amusing. She and Dale and Robert Jennings considered the
Cincinnati church campaign a challenge. It was one
they were eager to meet.

And so Fanny came to Cincinnati to rally the people
against what she called "priestcraft."

Frances Trollope was present in the courthouse on
that August night when Fanny delivered her first public
lecture. She saw dozens of people come forward to buy

subscriptions to the *New Harmony Gazette*. She wrote to mutual friends in Europe about Fanny's eloquence and new-found fame.

And then she added a note in her typically tart way: "*Something*, I know not what, *must* have befallen her when she followed Lafayette to America . . . . Fanny . . . has been delivering lectures on her favorite subjects of religion and marriage . . . . What her future fate will be, it is difficult to guess."

Chapter 20 **ON TOUR**

"Miss Wright . . . has with ruthless violence, broken loose from the restraints of decorum, which draw a circle round the life of women; . . . she has leaped over the boundary of feminine modesty."

LOUISVILLE FOCUS

"Public writers must feed popular prejudices, or cease to earn their bread by their profession."

FRANCES WRIGHT
AT LOUISVILLE

JEAN BADOLLET of Indiana wrote to his old friend Albert Gallatin in New York. Badollet was a veteran of the American Revolution, and a radical. He commented approvingly to Jefferson's former secretary of the treasury about Miss Frances Wright's activities.

"That remarkable woman," the one old veteran told the other, "is a deep and fearless thinker whose writing and lectures will go a great way towards unveiling the audacious schemes of the clergy and opposing a check to the flood of intolerant bigotry which threatens to overwhelm this land."

Badollet, all his life a supporter of the ideas of Thomas Paine and the French Revolution, thought she went a bit too far once in a while. But he added that "unlike the clergy, she does not . . . hurl us into damnation if we chance to dissent from her."

Gallatin, less of a radical than Badollet, did not extend his revolutionary ideas to include women's rights. "She ought not at all events to exhibit herself in a theatrical manner," he wrote back.

But most of Fanny's hearers were willing to put aside their prejudices against a woman giving public lectures in order to listen to her ideas. If they objected to her views on marriage, they did not let that fact interfere with their ardent support for her basic political philosophy: that the people should take their education and their government into their own hands without regard for the authority of the rich, the educated, or the pious; that they should change the existing institutions of American life and make them better, more democratic, more equal.

After Cincinnati, Fanny returned for a brief time to New Harmony before starting out on her lecture tour. She planned to sell subscriptions to the *New Harmony Gazette* as she traveled.

The *Gazette* was now Fanny's most important project. She and her young editorial staff were determined to make it the only American newspaper free of ties to either political party, and free also of religious influence.

Their goal was to expand its circulation and to put it on a paying basis. To do this, they needed an efficient production manager to take charge of printing.

New Harmony had ended its experiment in socialism and was now a colony of individual property owners. There was no future for the principal of the school, William Phiquepal D'Arusmont. The little educational reformer still had with him the three boys he had brought from France. He had promised their parents he would see to their education. Now he and they faced an uncertain future. Although he knew nothing about printing, Fanny and he agreed that he should become the newspaper's production manager.

"Mr. Phiquepal D'Arusmont," Fanny wrote later in her autobiography, "volunteered to acquire and communicate to his three pupils a thorough knowledge of the printing business in a month's time."

Despite his lack of experience, D'Arusmont was an intelligent and stubborn man, and he succeeded in mastering the necessary skills. After her Cincinnati lecture, Fanny had announced to the audience that a new issue of the *New Harmony Gazette* would be available on a certain date. "The paper arrived," she said, "on the day announced and was universally noticed for its general appearance and correctness of typography." Later all issues of the paper carried the notice: "Printed by William Phiquepal [D'Arusmont did not like to use his last name because he thought it sounded too aristocratic] and his pupils."

The name of the paper was also changed. It became

the *Free Enquirer.* "The title," wrote Dale in the first editorial of the new series, "has not been selected lightly. It expresses our intention; it marks our principles; it designates the character of our labor—Free Enquiry."

The little group from New Harmony separated in November. Camilla, who was pregnant, went with her husband to stay at Nashoba until the birth of her baby. Dale took over the full editorship of the *Enquirer* with D'Arusmont in charge of printing and mailing. Fanny and Robert Jennings, after leaving Camilla at Nashoba, boarded a river steamboat at Memphis and traveled up the Mississippi and Ohio rivers.

Their tour across the country was a triumphant procession. Wherever they went, they drew great crowds of listeners and supporters. But their success was measured in more than applause. From each town they sent back lists of new subscribers to the *Free Enquirer,* together with the dollars they had contributed to pay for the paper. It was quickly becoming a well-known, widely read weekly.

In Louisville Fanny lectured in the Richmond Theater. The hall was so crowded that the balconies seemed about to sink under the weight of the crowd. Someone cried, *"Fire!"* The crowd—half of them women defying the prejudice against their presence in a theater—almost panicked. Only the presence of mind and the coolness of a few level-headed people calmed the frightened audience and kept them from rushing to the exits and trampling each other.

"Among these few stood Frances Wright," said an

eye-witness, "calm, tranquil and collected . . . . Her example influenced many of the ladies in the boxes and on the stage . . . ."

In Louisville, as in Cincinnati, the press attacked her and printed letters from hostile readers. They printed nothing about what she actually said, or about the size of the crowds that came to hear her. They ignored the near panic in the Richmond Theater and the fact that the large crowd applauded her enthusiastically.

This confirmed her conviction of the importance of the *Free Enquirer.* Social reformers and radicals could not expect fair treatment from the press. They would have to rely on their own newspaper.

From Louisville, Fanny and Jennings went across the mountains by stagecoach. They passed through Wheeling, West Virginia, where they lectured, and finally arrived in Baltimore. Here they were met by Dr. Haslam, the leader of the local liberals.

The doctor insisted that Fanny and Jennings spend the night in his home and not in a hotel. There had been rumors of mob violence, talk of breaking up the lecture meeting. Fanny had been winning fame, but she had also been arousing resentment. This resentment came not only from religious people or from people with conservative opinions. It came from those who hated and feared women's equality. They objected to a woman's speaking in public.

Even some who agreed with her views attacked her for being "unnatural" and "unfeminine." A woman's place, they said, was in the home taking care of her family. For a woman to prefer a public career to marriage, as Fanny apparently did, seemed abnormal.

One letter writer said she ought to stay home and have a family. He quoted Napoleon Bonaparte's answer to a question about who was the greatest woman who ever lived: "She that has had the most children."

Fanny called that "an excellent reply for Bonaparte!" And then she added her own opinion: "I consider her 'the greatest woman' who will best assist in justly educating children . . . the taking care of one family would be doing less good than the encouraging the heads of all families to enquire how they may best take care of theirs."

The newspapers printed crude insults. They called her "priestess of Beelzebub," "female monster," "masculine," and "unnatural." Their favorite word of attack was "infidel." To these she paid no attention at all.

In fact, there was no trouble in Baltimore. Perhaps this was because of her calm and confident manner. She began by assuring her audience that since they were American gentlemen she was certain they would be both courteous and attentive.

They were more than that. They were enthusiastic for the five successive nights she lectured there. Among her most interested listeners were a large number of Quakers. They were followers of the dissenting liberal Quaker preacher Elias Hicks. He taught a personal religion, in which each person listened only to his own conscience and did what he personally thought was right and moral. To the Hicksite Quakers Fanny's ideas about free inquiry seemed familiar and agreeable.

From Baltimore, she went to Philadelphia. She had been turning over in her mind the thought of settling in one of the eastern cities where religious influence was strong. She felt encouraged enough to challenge the powerful conservative establishment. The election of Jackson had contributed to the new hopeful mood of radicals and reformers everywhere.

"Baltimore," she wrote to Camilla, "has been the stronghold of priestcraft for some years past, and the churches are more spacious and costly than in any city of the union." But she thought she should see Philadelphia and New York before deciding.

After Philadelphia she set out for New York. It was the city where everything in America was the *most*. It had the strongest reformers, the most powerful conservatives, the biggest thieves, and the most radical workers. New York, she wrote, was "the head seat at once of popular energy, sectarian and clerical wealth and power, and financial and political corruption."

New York was the cockpit of America. There political and intellectual battles were the most bitter. If the free enquirers succeeded in New York, they would succeed on the grandest scale. If they failed, they failed forever.

On New Year's Eve 1828, Fanny stood on the deck of the New York ferry in the cold winter darkness. The boat left the New Jersey side and moved toward the

gaslights of New York. It moved toward people she had
loved and cherished, people who had cared for her
when she first came from England a little more than ten
years earlier, a young woman of twenty-three. Everyone
had loved her in those days.

Now her name was a curse and a red flag to some, a
shining inspiration to others. Some of her old friends
might understand her notoriety. Some might not, but
they would keep silent. "Others," she thought soberly,
"might feel embarrassed."

Chapter 21 **NEW YORK**

"This is truly the stronghold of superstition or rather of craft. Baltimore is nothing to it. A priest at every step and a score of churches in every street, all apostrophizing and excommunicating the 'Female Monster'."

FRANCES WRIGHT

THE last time she had been in New York, Lafayette had also been there. It had been a time of pomp and glory. The whole city had turned out to honor the general. She had had her portrait painted by the fashionable artist Henry Inman.

Now she came to New York bringing conflict and controversy.

At first only the liberals and freethinkers of the city paid any attention to her. There was a free-thought club in New York. They held an annual banquet on the birthday of Thomas Paine. They published a free-thought newspaper, the *New York Correspondent*, on which Richard Jennings had been a reporter. Robert Owen (the elder) and Fanny Wright were among their heroes. And now Fanny had come to town!

Jennings opened an office for the sale of subscriptions to the paper. Fanny scheduled six lectures, rented the hall, and paid the bill. She insisted, as usual, that the lectures be free.

On Saturday, January 3, at about seven o'clock, Fanny stood on the platform of Masonic Hall and delivered her first lecture. Jennings had escorted her to the podium, taken her hat and cloak, and left her there. Four or five Quaker women sat protectively behind her. She had become popular with the Hicksite Quakers, and a committee of their women went with her to all her public lectures.

Fanny wore a dark blouse with a white ruff. She stood and looked out at the audience. It was jammed to capacity with more than fifteen hundred people. Some friends from her early New York days sat conspicuously in front. There was Cadwallader Colden, the conservative former mayor. And there was Dr. William McNevin, the old Irish friend of Rabina Millar and Wolfe Tone.

Charles Wilkes was not there. Her financial adviser had broken with her. She had sent him a note graciously offering to find another watchdog for her property. He had graciously accepted.

The audience was the most enthusiastic of any she had met. There were not many Quakers, but many radical workingmen and young mechanics. They wanted the ten-hour working day. They wanted an end to the law that put a man in jail if he could not pay his bills. Above all, they wanted their own way in politics now that they could vote.

One of the radical New York workingmen who went to Fanny's lectures and loved every word she said was a Brooklyn carpenter named Walter Whitman. He had three sons: Thomas Jefferson Whitman, Andrew Jackson Whitman, and Walter Whitman, Jr.

That first night in New York the press was curious rather than unfriendly. The *Commercial Advertiser* found much to praise.

"Her voice," said the *Advertiser*'s reporter, "which filled the room without apparent effort on the part of the speaker, is both strong and sweet. We recollect no female whose recitations in this city have been celebrated, at all comparable to this lady, in particular. Her enunciation is perfect . . . her gestures appropriate and graceful . . . . we believe she is unrivalled by any of the public speakers in this city."

The *Advertiser* said little or nothing about the ideas she expressed except that she seemed to be professing some sort of "infidelity." This was the word used to describe the ideas of those who were critics of organized religion.

The *Evening Post* was a Democratic paper, supporting Andrew Jackson. Although its editor, the poet William Cullen Bryant, had some liberal ideas he was quite hostile to equality for women. He was also suspicious of the radical Democrats in his party. He poked fun at Fanny in a poem describing her as:

The new Aspasia
From whom Religion awaits her doom.

Aspasia was the beautiful mistress of Pericles, the statesman of ancient Athens. She was also his political adviser and was noted for her intelligence and her lack of religious faith. Fanny could not have been offended at the comparison.

Her first lecture in New York encouraged her to settle there. The applause and support she received were tremendous. There was little or no hostility. There were no attempts to break up her meetings. "Dearest love," she wrote to Camilla, "we are about to pitch our tent here."

By her third lecture, when she had warmed up and gotten around to attacking the clergy, the New York press felt differently about her. Perhaps they were angered also at the news that she was bringing the *Free Enquirer* to town and expected to publish it in the city from that time on. The *New York Correspondent* was going bankrupt, and there was a need now for a lively free-thought paper.

One week after it had found her language "singularly well chosen and accurate," the *Commercial Advertiser* called her "a bold blasphemer and a voluptuous preacher of licentiousness." The *New York American* said of her that when she expresses the ideas she holds "she ceases to be a woman, and is no longer ought else than what we have taken the liberty of calling her—a female monster."

The *Post* called itself a liberal paper. Yet it went so

far as to almost advocate violence and arson in an attempt to stop her from speaking. When it heard that Fanny had rented the Park Theater—the same theater where *Altorf* had first been produced in 1819—for a second series of lectures, it asked: "Suppose . . . that a riot should ensue, which should end in the demolition of the interior of the building, or even in burning it down, on whom would the loss fall? Would the policy of insurance against fire . . . cover the loss?" The *Post* also asked if the public authorities ought not to forbid the meeting as a threat to public order. Yet the only mention of violence, fire, and bloodshed had come from the pages of the *Post.*

The night of the next meeting in Masonic Hall, with the audience two thirds women and girls, an attempt was made to burn down the building. A barrel filled with oil of turpentine and other inflammable materials was set afire and rolled into the main entrance. The good order of the audience and the quick action of some young mechanics who had made themselves Fanny's unofficial bodyguard kept the blaze from spreading.

The following Sunday a lecture by the Universalist minister Abner Kneeland, a free enquirer despite the fact that he was a clergyman, was broken up when someone turned off the gas that lit the hall. Two thousand people sat calmly in the dark until they were able to leave the building. The free enquirers and their supporters were convinced that the churches were behind the arson at Masonic Hall and the turning off of the gas at Kneeland's lecture.

When the time approached for Fanny's first lecture in the Park Theater, the *Post* repeated its invitation to violence. A notice in that paper said it was sorry to hear that Frances Wright "persists in her determination." It added, "We hope nothing will happen of a dangerous or even unpleasant nature."

In fact nothing unpleasant or dangerous did happen. Popular support for Fanny and her ideas was too great. Thousands of people turned out at every lecture, and almost all of them came to cheer. It was impossible to stir mob violence against her in New York. The only attacks that could be launched were sermons from church pulpits or editorials by newspaper editors. These she welcomed.

Even the management of the Park Theater refused to be intimidated. They knew Fanny was popular enough to bring them good business. They not only rented her the building for lectures all through January and February; they even revived *Altorf* and made money with two successful performances.

To Fanny the actions of the press confirmed her decision to establish the *Free Enquirer* in New York. She sent word for Dale and D'Arusmont to come as soon as they could. She found a radical printer, George Evans. The *Free Enquirer* was a labor of love for him. He risked his regular customers to print free-thought literature. He was a passionate follower of the ideas of Tom Paine. She assigned Robert Jennings to be editor. In the first

New York edition of the paper, she took off after one of her favorite enemies.

"In the present state of the American press," she wrote in a signed editorial in the *Free Enquirer* for January 21, "it is hard to judge who are in the side of truth. Nay, were we to take the press for an organ of public sentiment we might conceive that a mental palsy had fallen upon the nation . . . . But the press does not speak the voice of the nation. It does not even speak the voice of those who write for it . . . ."

What infuriated her enemies most was her following through on her own advice: buy a church and turn it into a hall of science. She did exactly that, convinced that independent-minded people could only educate themselves and express themselves if they owned their own press and their own meeting hall.

Using seven thousand dollars of her money, she bought the Ebenezer Church in Broome Street and renamed it the Hall of Science. After remodeling, it would seat twelve hundred people. The *Free Enquirer* offices were in the basement. True to her principles, she tried to run it as a cooperative with five trustees. Here lectures would be given; a secular Sunday school set up, and a bookstore selling the works of Thomas Paine, Mary Wollstonecraft, and other radical thinkers. Other organizations could rent the building for meetings of their own.

When she came to New York on New Year's Eve there appeared to be only a handful of nonreligious people in the city. Now, only months later, there seemed to be thousands. New York was decidedly the place for her work.

Fanny rented a large comfortable house from Richard Riker, the recorder of the city of New York. It was on the East River a few miles from downtown New York, near the village of Yorkville, at what is now East Seventy-fifth Street. It had a farm with cows and a garden. The rent for the entire property was $440 a year.

There Fanny and her companions—Jennings, Dale, D'Arusmont and his three boys, and later Camilla—lived economically. They saved on expenses by going without tea, coffee, and sugar, and by eating very little meat. They had plenty of vegetables from the garden, plenty of milk from the cows. Butter was sixteen cents a pound, so they made their own. Flour, to make bread, was five dollars a barrel.

Their total expenses, including living expenses and the cost of printing the *Free Enquirer*, came to three thousand dollars a year. That was exactly the income they received from their one thousand paid subscribers, at three dollars a year each.   "There we lived," Dale remembered in his old age, "and there our paper was handsomely printed by three lads who had been trained in the New Harmony printing office. They boarded with us, and we paid them a dollar a week each. They got out the paper in five days of the week, and we paid them for extra work, when they did any.

"Though it was a somewhat hard and self-denying life, my recollections would prompt me to say that I was bright and cheerful through it all."

The times were bright and cheerful for all reformers. President Jackson and his supporters planned to make many changes. They intended to restrict the power of big businessmen and limit the churches' influence in American life. They were sympathetic to the needs of those who most wanted change—workingmen, mechanics, farmers, and small businessmen.

Chapter 22 THE *FREE ENQUIRER*

"The paper [is] empty, insignificant, and tedious . . . Its imbecile dullness render[s] it harmlessly wicked."
NEW YORK COM-
MERCIAL ADVERTISER

"The New York Free Enquirer *I think amongst the best publications in the United States."*
JEAN BADOLLET

THE *Free Enquirer* lasted only a few years. But for most of that time, and especially during the period when Fanny, Dale Owen, and Robert Jennings were its editors, it was a lively, popular, interesting weekly. It had humor as well as political argument. It kept its eye out for any unusual bit of news that seemed to make a point. Often the point was directed against organized religion.

A Vermont publisher advertised cheap copies of the Bible—"much cheaper than the American Bible Society"—because he printed them by water power. He offered a free copy to every poor person who said he wanted to read it but couldn't afford to buy it.

The *Free Enquirer* published his notice and added the comment: "We have always been friendly to the general circulation of the Bible in all Christian countries; knowing that the more it is read, the better it can be judged."

A reader wrote to say that it was hard to accept the story of Jonah and the whale. Fanny's answer was to quote the remark that "it was surely but an easy miracle, that of a whale swallowing Jonah, seeing that so many human beings are swallowing both Jonah and the whale every day."

Sometimes it seemed as if the *Free Enquirer* went out of its way to attack religion. The paper printed the obituary of a Mrs. Elizabeth Bartine, who had become a free enquirer shortly before her death. When she heard the doctor speak to her husband about getting a clergyman to visit her and pray over her, she said, according to the *Free Enquirer*: "I have lived long happily without a priest—I wish to die peaceably without one. And, when dead, if the doctor wishes to open my body, let him do so. It may be of service to the living."

Much of the *Free Enquirer* was taken up in this way. There were learned articles on theology. There were excerpts from the writings of such freethinkers as Thomas Paine, Ethan Allen, and Richard Carlile. Paine's *Age of Reason* was frequently advertised. So were the works of Voltaire and of other anticlerical philosophers.

The climate of American public opinion was becoming favorable to the *Free Enquirer*'s ideas. The Democratic party was also opposed to the effort to compel observance of the Christian religion. When some religious leaders tried to get President Jackson to proclaim a national day of prayer during a cholera epidemic, he refused. Senator Richard Johnson, a Democrat from Kentucky, was the leading congressional opponent of the Sabbath observance laws.

The General Union for Promoting the Observance of the Christian Sabbath, a new organization formed in 1828, worried independent-minded Christians as well as Jews and nonbelievers. This organization wanted to introduce religious textbooks into the public schools. It sought to inject religion into education.

Working-class parents objected. They looked upon the schools as the only ladder of opportunity by which their children might climb up in the world. They wanted their children to learn mathematics, science, grammar, and other useful subjects. Church-controlled schools appeared to be an obstacle to their ambition for their children.

The young mechanics and factory workers saw the religious revival movement as a threat to their demands for shorter hours, higher wages, and better working conditions. Its newspapers were hostile to their needs. Its clergymen preached sermons telling them to rely on prayer. Whenever workers went on strike, religious leaders opposed them and sided with the factory owners.

The Great Revival in religion was strong in New York state, especially in the north and west. Its fanati-

cism and intolerance frightened many people. It seemed
suspiciously like the religious repression that had forced
the original colonists—their ancestors—to flee England.
Liberal Christians felt threatened. "It is seriously believed by the enlightened and liberal of all denomina-
tions," said one Unitarian paper, "that the Presbyterians and other 'Orthodox' Clergy have been maneu-
vering for years to effect an unholy union between
Church and state . . . ."

To all these people, to those raised in the tradition of
Thomas Jefferson and James Madison, organized religion was a dangerous enemy. Even former President
John Quincy Adams was not safe and had to be defended, in the *Free Enquirer*, from the accusation of not
observing the Sabbath. In this atmosphere the paper
seemed to be a fresh breeze of free opinion. It printed
controversial ideas that other papers ignored. It reported events that other papers suppressed.

The *Free Enquirer* was especially popular with workingmen. One of these was Walter Whitman, the father
of the poet Walt Whitman. He was a subscriber to the
paper.

Fanny attracted women readers by her articles on
marriage, family life, and womens' rights. When Pennsylvania passed a divorce law she wrote an angry editorial, even though she thought women should have the
right to leave their husbands.

"Men and women permitted by act of the states to
live apart!" she wrote. Ridiculous! The marriage law
gives fees to clergymen, she said. Now we shall have a

law that will give fees to lawyers. "An excuse to legislators for taking the people's money."

She had contempt for all laws attempting to regulate love, morality, and marriage. "We can never regulate the affections of men and women," she wrote. She also said that "if laws could make a nation honest, truly the Americans were the most honest of all the Nations upon the Earth!" She sometimes supported new laws that corrected old injustices. But if she had her way, there would be fewer laws, not more.

When Massachusetts passed a law allowing a divorced woman to get back her own property "which her husband received by reason of the marriage," she wrote with bitter sarcasm: "Now is it not marvelous that in the nineteenth century, and in this country, such an act of the legislature should have been necessary?"

Women wrote to her about their problems. One young woman with three children and a husband who was a drunkard wrote to the *Free Enquirer*: "I feel able to bring up these three little cherubs in decency, were I to have no more." But what should she do to keep from having more children? "I can see no other alternative left for me than to tear myself away from the man . . . or continue, and bring into existence a numerous family of helpless and destitute . . . . I do hope and believe you will give me such advice and counsel as to your own daughter."

Fanny's comment, written in the spring of 1829, sounds surprisingly modern. She called the bringing of unwanted children into the world "the most criminal of all activities." But she blamed neither the mother nor the father.

She blamed instead the educational system "which leaves the youth of either sex in ignorance" about how babies are conceived and born. Instead of leading young people to virtue through reason, she said, education actually reinforces ignorance.

She went on to discuss the problem of having too many children. "Should not all women in a similar situation consider whether they can consistently . . . give birth to children who must inevitably be doomed to a life of ignorance and consequent vice and misery?"

Why, she asked, are people who are unfit to be parents enabled to produce children "simply because they take out a priest's permit for the same?"

As to the woman with the alcoholic husband: "Why should not a woman be encouraged to choose none but a suitable father for her children, and to leave her companion when he becomes unsuitable?"

Fanny's answer also took up the question of unlimited population growth. She criticized American and English parents for not paying more attention to the problem caused by having more children than the community can afford.

"The French are very extensively careful to limit their progeny," she noted. "It is true that this country could admit of a much larger increase of population than [Europe] but . . . under existing arrangements the population is already distressed."

The *Free Enquirer* was probably the only paper in the

United States—perhaps in the whole world—in which one could read about birth control, the marriage rights of women, and the population explosion. This did not make it popular with everyone. Fanny did not fool herself about that. "Truths such as these," she concluded, "are unsavory."

The paper did not ignore lighter news or commonplace events. It printed a long essay reporting the medical hazards of wearing the new stiff corsets made of whalebone. Under the title "Fashionable Incarceration," it printed pages of symptoms and diseases attributed to "tight lacing." The article concluded: "All this torture, uneasiness, and inconvenience is patiently endured, and for what? because it is fashionable!"

For some militant women of 1829 the corset was as much a symbol of oppression as the brassiere is to some militant women today.

The *Free Enquirer* also printed statistical information, excerpts from other newspapers, resolutions passed by workingmen's organizations and free-thought clubs, and Fanny Wright's lectures.

It published poems by Byron and Shelley; sometimes it published poems by Fanny. It advertised club meetings, lectures, Hall of Science programs, ran the advertisements of tradesmen, shopkeepers, professional people, legal notices, and announcements of new books.

It did not limit itself to Fanny's pet subjects. "We had other heresies which brought us reproach," said Robert Dale Owen. "We advocated the abolition of imprisonment for debt and of capital punishment; equality for women, social, pecuniary and political; equality of civil rights for all persons without distinction of color; and the right of every man to testify in a court of justice without inquiry being made as to his religious creed.

"Above all, we urged the importance of a national system of education, free from sectarian teachings, with industrial schools where the children of the poor might be taught farming or a trade, and obtain, without charge, support as well as education.

"This last brought upon us the imputation of favoring communism."

Chapter 23 HALL OF
SCIENCE

*"All things may we hope for man,
should our efforts in this place be
successful."*

FRANCES WRIGHT

On September 15, 1829, Philadelphia free enquirers
rented the Walnut Street Theater for seventy-five dollars and invited Fanny to come and lecture. September
15 was a Sunday night, the only night when the theater
—the biggest public hall in the city—was available.

Advertisements were sent out. Notices announcing
the time and place of the lecture were posted. But suddenly the theater owners said that renting their property
for money on a Sunday was a violation of a city ordi-
nance forbidding the doing of business on the Sabbath.
They ordered the manager to cancel the rental agreement.

The manager offered to let Fanny speak in the theater
free of charge. The owners refused.

Fanny's friends then rented Washington Hall, a

smaller building, from the wife of its owner, who was out of town. Again public notices went out.

Pressure was now put on Mrs. Labbe, the wife of the owner of Washington Hall. She was threatened with arrest for violation of the Sabbath. She was warned that there might be riots in her theater. She was advised that it might be set afire. Her husband's regular customers threatened to do no more business with him.

Mrs. Labbe became frightened, but not frightened enough to cancel her agreement to rent the theater. Still, Fanny's friends felt they ought to do so of their own accord. They did not want Mrs. Labbe to suffer.

Sunday morning, with Fanny already on her way, a committee of two hundred of the leading liberals and free enquirers of Philadelphia met in Military Hall, a public building, to discuss what they should do. The committee decided to hold the meeting that night in that very hall.

By six o'clock crowds had begun to form at both the Walnut Street Theater and Washington Hall. When they were told there would be no Fanny Wright lecture in either place, they refused to believe it. They became angry and restless. Finally, delegates had to come from the committee to tell them that Fanny would indeed lecture at Military Hall later in the evening.

By seven o'clock the streets were a great tangle—a scene of chaos and confusion. Knots of people milled about exchanging rumors as to whether Fanny would or would not lecture that night.

Fanny described the confusion in an article in the *Free Enquirer.* "Information being brought to me of the existing and increasing excitement, I drove to the spot accompanied by some male friends . . . . When the carriage approached, the multitude who thronged the surrounding streets and open space between the Hall and the United States bank quietly gave way, until this became impossible from the increasing density of the crowd."

Unable to get any closer, Fanny stood up in her carriage. "It appears to me impossible to gain entrance to the Hall, or to deliver any lecture tonight," she announced, "except in the open air. To this my lungs are unequal, and I must decline." She said that a hall would be rented for a weekday, and she would return to Philadelphia at that time and speak.

Then she drew a moral for her listeners. "It is absolutely necessary that the People should have a Hall of their own, for the use of public lectures, from which they could not be excluded either by the Clergy or the Aristocracy."

The Hall of Science on Broome Street in New York was such a hall. For its few brief years of life, it was an important community center for liberal, free-thinking New Yorkers. On Sunday mornings its school offered courses for men and women in arithmetic, mathematics, anatomy, natural history, physics, chemistry, geometry, reading, writing, composing, and public speaking. Admission was free. The services of a physician and a public dispensary were soon added.

A month later the Hall of Science Day School began offering "an English education" at a fee of five dollars for each quarter of the academic year. In a short while the hall attracted so many students that an admission charge of twenty-five cents was instituted. The Sunday school was still free for regular pupils; visitors could observe for twelve and a half cents.

The Hall of Science earned its own way and brought a bit extra into the commune at Riker's farm. An admission fee of ten cents was charged for the regular Sunday lectures. Fees for rentals to other speakers and organizations came in occasionally. The bookstore sold two thousand dollars' worth of liberal and radical publications in its first year.

In addition to Sunday lectures by Fanny, Robert Dale Owen, or Robert Jennings, the hall was available to the public for meetings of "scientific purpose."

The Hall of Science was the only place in the United States in the 1820's and 30's where a young mechanic or workingman could get any sort of higher education. Its library, its public debates, its meeting halls were always available. Fanny's lecture fees provided the larger part of its income. At the hall young men and women heard discussion of the ideas of Thomas Paine and other radical democrats. For the working-class youth who were barred from higher education because they had no money, the hall was a college campus.

Fanny addressed many of her lectures and newspaper articles to the young mechanics of New York. They in turn were among her most fervent admirers. In one of her last Hall of Science lectures she told such an audience of the importance of learning how to speak properly in public in order to influence others. "To the young," she added, "do I look for most zeal in the cause of reform . . . ."

The Hall of Science played an important part in the development of that zeal for reform. Out of it came a new political organization, the Working Men's Party, and its newspaper, *The Working Man's Advocate.*

Chapter 24 THE NEW YORK
WORKING MEN'S
PARTY

*"We do not believe there can be a single person found
east of the mountains who ever thanked God for permission to work in a cotton mill."*

SETH LUTHER, "ADDRESS TO THE
WORKING MEN OF NEW ENGLAND"

*"All children are entitled to equal education; all adults
to equal property; and all mankind to equal privileges."*

MOTTO OF *THE
WORKING MAN'S ADVOCATE*

FANNY'S greatest notoriety was associated with her leadership of the New York Working Men's Party—one of
the first labor parties in the United States. This new political party arose out of the grievances of the city's
wage earners. One of their bitterest complaints was
against the law that put a man in debtors' prison if he
could not pay his bills.

On the last day of the year 1829 the prisoners in cell number 3, New York Debtors' Prison, sent a petition to City Sheriff James Shaw. The petition said: "Be good enough to call and see us as we have certain things to communicate to you."

Attached to the petition was the following list of complaints:

That at eight o'clock one evening the keeper had refused medical aid to a prisoner groaning in agony from severe stomach pains. "This is no time to get a doctor," said the keeper. "You should have thought of that in the daytime." When it was pointed out to him that the man had no pains in the daytime, and that if he did not get treatment soon he might die, the keeper said: "Let him die."

That when a woman came to see her husband in jail, "the keeper handled her in a very immodest and indecent manner . . . in a way which decency forbids us to explain." When she complained, the keeper dared her to tell her husband.

That the doors of the jail were open to the public for only short periods each day. Since friends and relatives had to bring the prisoners their food (the Debtors' Prison did not feed them) they might go hungry for days if they were not visited at the prescribed time.

There is no record of what followed the petition to Sheriff Shaw. But for the men in cell number 3, and for the two thousand other debtors in jail in New York City that year, the greatest grievance of all had not even been mentioned. That was the debtors' law itself. This law put a man in jail if he owed money and could not pay it. Not being able to pay one's bills was a crime. Sometimes owing as little as two or three dollars was enough to put a man in jail. There he stayed until his family or friends could raise the money.

Only poor men went to prison for owing money. For their families, left without income, this could mean disaster. A worker who owned nothing but what he earned by the labor of his hands usually had no savings.

A man with property had no trouble paying his bills and staying out of jail. He could get loans from banks. That was what banks were for—to provide credit for rich people.

The young mechanics and workingmen demanded the abolition of the law putting a man in jail for debt. Fanny and Dale and their fellow workers on the *Free Enquirer* supported that demand.

There were other injustices. Their grandfathers had fought for freedom and equality in 1776. But now, in 1829, the children of the poor did not get an education equal to that of the children of the rich. In New York there were no free public schools for them to go to.

For some poor children there were charity or "common" schools supported by churches. These provided no real education in useful subjects, such as reading or arithmetic. For the vast majority of poor children there was no system of education at all, but for the children of the rich there were private schools, and later colleges and universities.

Close to one million American children between the

ages of five and fifteen did not go to school. All of them grew up without ever learning how to read and write. In New York City alone there were about twenty-five thousand children who had no schooling.

"We consider it an exclusive privilege for one portion of the community to have the means of education in colleges," said the paper, *The Working Man's Advocate*, in its first issue, "while another is restricted to common schools or perhaps by extreme poverty, even deprived of the limited education to be acquired in those establishments. Our voice, therefore, shall be raised in favor of a system of education which shall be equally open to all, as in a real republic it should be."

The Working Man's Advocate carried on its masthead the legend *Edited By a Mechanic*. The "mechanic" was George Evans, who had been the printer of the *Free Enquirer* before William Phiquepal D'Arusmont and his three pupils had come to New York to live on the farm with Fanny and Robert Dale Owen. Evans was an old friend and supporter of Fanny's. From the very start the staffs of the *Enquirer* and the *Advocate* were allies and friends.

The *Advocate* spoke for the new political organization that the more radical mechanics and workers were forming in New York. They called it the Working Men's Party.

The workingman was worried by the change from hand labor to machine labor. What this change meant to him was best described by another labor newspaper, the *Mechanic's Free Press* of Philadelphia:

"The owners of one kind of machine can exchange their products for the products of other machines; *but what is to become of those who have no machines of their own?* Will any one employ them? Will they have anything to give in exchange for their supplies? Must they not become paupers as they are becoming now? Or be annihilated by starvation as some have recommended that they be? Or turn robbers? . . . Before the working people can be benefitted by machines they must be proprietors of machines. But they can never be proprietors until the present forced system of inequality is done away, or until there is a better mode of distribution."

The workingmen had many complaints. They objected to the fact that church property was exempt from taxation. They objected to the fact that they had to serve in the state militia, and that if they did not turn out for duty they were put in jail. If the rich did not turn out, they had only to pay fines.

The workingmen objected to the fact that strikes and unions were forbidden by law. They objected to the banking system which lent money to the rich and offered nothing to the poor. They objected to the fact that they were often paid their wages in goods—in barrels of wheat or yards of cloth—or in paper scrip, instead of cash they could exchange for whatever they needed.

They objected to attempts to make them work more than ten hours a day. "Ten hours, well and faithfully employed," they said in a resolution reported in the

Free Enquirer, "is as much as an employer ought to receive or require for a day's work."

The United States of America, the freest land in the world, was now forty years old. Workingmen now had the right to vote. But it was a right that seemed to have little value.

"What advantage, fellow workmen," said a public statement of the Working Men's Political Association of Northern Philadelphia, "have we ever derived from the acts of those whom our suffrages have elevated to the important and honorable post of legislators? Can anyone point to a single law in the statute book of this commonwealth calculated to benefit the working classes? There is no such law."

Politicians got elected with workers' votes and then passed laws that benefited businessmen—laws licensing taverns and lotteries, laws protecting monopolies, laws incorporating businesses—but no laws that dealt with the workingmen's problems.

The New York Working Men's Party had many supporters—many thousands of workingmen who formed the majority of the voters in some districts of the city. They had support also from middle-class liberals and reformers. Robert Dale Owen, George Evans, Robert Jennings, and especially Fanny Wright were active supporters of the new party. Fanny Wright had concluded that if the Working Men's Party won political power in the state her ideas about public education could be carried out.

High up in Andrew Jackson's Democratic party the

workingmen also had friends. The man they looked to with the most hope was Senator Richard Johnson. He had led the fight against the Sabbath observance law and the fight against imprisonment for debt.

But many other Democrats feared the Working Men's Party would take votes away from their own candidates. In New York City the Democratic leaders of the Tammany Club fought bitterly against the new party. So did the conservative National Republicans.

Chapter 25 **THE ELECTION
OF 1829**

*"Experience teaches that we have nothing to hope
from the aristocrats of society and that our only
course to pursue is to send men of our own description, if we can, to the Legislature at Albany."*
RESOLUTION OF THE NEW YORK
WORKING MEN'S PARTY

FANNY had two opinions about the new political party.

She did not agree with the view that working people
constituted a separate class. She thought that all human
beings belonged to one class—the great human family.

"I object to the title of *working men*," she told a meeting of young mechanics, "and yet more to that of a
'working man's *party.*' " Why should people be "parti-
tioned off into classes, and arrayed against each other?"
She told them she did not want them to assume that she
considered "their interests distinct from those of other
classes of the community."

On the other hand she had come to the conclusion
that only people who worked with their hands were capable of bringing about changes in America. They were

the largest single group in the population. They were the
ones who had the most to gain from reform.

"I do look to the industrious classes, generally and especially, but by no means *exclusively*, for the salvation
of the country . . . . So far as reform may be practica-
ble . . . it is more likely to be effectually promoted by
the classes who *directly suffer* than by those who *immediately live* by the errors and abuses. . . ."

Fanny, Dale, and the other free enquirers threw their
talents into the election campaign. The Working Men's
Party ran candidates for all ten New York City seats in
the state Assembly. All but one, a doctor, were men
who worked with their hands. There were two machin-
ists, two carpenters, a painter, a printer, a barrelmaker,
a grocer, and a foundry worker.

The nominations were made a week before Election
Day. The party had only seventy-five dollars in its campaign treasury, but it had popular issues to campaign
on: abolition of imprisonment for debt, free public
schools, and a mechanics' lien law that guaranteed a
worker his wages in cash.

The election was a hard-fought one. Thousands more
voters came to the polls than had been expected. The
poor people, who had only recently won the right to
vote but who had often not bothered to use that right,
found themselves caught up in the excitement. Politics
had meaning for them. A total of seventy thousand people voted in the city, so many that three days instead of
one had to be set aside to accommodate the balloting.

There were street riots and mass meetings. There

were charges of illegal voting. The leaders of the Democratic party and the National Republican party were
frightened by the prospects of the Working Men's Party
winning voters. Their papers attacked Working Men's
supporters as "Fanny Wrightmen." They made fun of
them for following the leadership of a woman. They accused the party of godlessness.

One of the newspapers raked up the stories about
Richardson and his black wife Josephine. They reprinted Fanny's comments about marriage. They talked
about her free-love colony in Nashoba. They circulated
her earlier opinions about mixing the black and white
races.

Fanny and Robert Dale Owen chose this inopportune
time to put forward their new idea for a national education system.

Fanny had never wavered from her original conviction that real change could come about only through
a radically new system of education. It was the special
school at New Harmony that had attracted her. It was
D'Arusmont's position as principal of that school and
his views as an educational reformer that interested her
in him. Reeducation of the children of black slaves and
of white masters had been at the heart of her Nashoba
plan.

Now she was convinced that a new educational plan
was the key to the problems of the poor and the workingman. Once all the children of the next generation
had been freed from the class prejudice, religious preju-

dices, and racial prejudices of their parents a happy new America could be built.

There would be no need in such an America to fight for the abolition of imprisonment for debt, or for the ten-hour day, or for public schools. One would not have to find ways to help blacks. Compulsory Sabbath observance would not exist. Women would be liberated, and would enjoy equality with men.

But to accomplish this reeducation of the American people, the present system of schooling would have to be replaced, not improved. In the first place, said Fanny and Dale, even free public schooling could never help the children of the poor. As long as their parents could not feed or clothe them properly, no amount of education would do them any good.

In the second place, they said, how could one trust ordinary schoolteachers to do the job and teach the truth? "They dare not speak that which by endangering their popularity would endanger their fortunes," said Fanny. They have to teach "not what is true but what is palatable." Palatable, she added, to the clergymen, to the press, to the rich, and to the politicians who employ teachers and pay their salaries.

But the biggest problem was the parents. How could one raise a new generation different from the old if the children went back to their families each night and learned the same old hatreds and prejudices? The children would grow up to be just like their mothers and fathers no matter what kind of schooling they had.

Unless they could be separated from their parents—
this was Fanny's idea. In order to break the unending
chain, in which each generation raises the next to repeat
the same mistakes, Fanny and Dale proposed a new educational plan. Under this plan children would be taken
from their parents at an early age and educated in national boarding schools at government expense until
they reached maturity. They would also be fed, clothed,
and cared for at government expense.

Parents could visit their children, but they could not
take them away, and they could not interfere in their
education. All children would be treated alike regard-
less of sex or color. There would be no distinctions.
They would wear the same clothing, do the same class
work, and eat the same food.

There would be no religious instruction. The knowledge taught would be only that which was obtained by
observation through the senses. Fanny's Epicurean philosophy was, in addition to Dale's experimental ideas
concerning education, the guiding spirit of this new educational scheme. "It would be an education," said
Fanny, "free for all and at the expense of all . . . a state
system of equal, protective, republican and universal
education . . . ."

Fanny and Dale brought these ideas into the Working Men's Party. They added them to the party's other
demands.

Some of the workingmen agreed with this plan. The
painters' union went on record supporting it.

Most of the workingmen, however, were suspicious. They did not care for the idea of having their children taken away from their control. In fact, most of them were not interested in changing America. What they wanted were specific measures like the abolition of imprisonment for debt.

A small number of the workingmen were followers of the radical machinist Thomas Skidmore, one of the leaders of the New York Working Men's Party. Skidmore was a passionate believer in the ideas of Thomas Paine. He had written a book, *The Rights of Man to Property*. He believed that all property should be taken away from its owners and divided up so that every man over the age of twenty-one and every unmarried woman would receive 160 acres to keep, provided they worked it themselves and did not rent it or sell it. He objected to the right of private property. Skidmore also thought that women and blacks should have the right to vote.

During the election campaign Fanny was out of New York City, lecturing in Utica, Schenectady, and other upstate cities. She was more concerned with her long-range plans to change America—especially with publicizing her national education plan—than with the results of the election. Dale stayed behind to put out the *Free Enquirer*.

She was trapped in Buffalo by a heavy snowfall at election time. Finally the news from New York reached her. The Working Men's Party had elected one member·

to the state assembly and had polled more than six thousand votes for each of its candidates, except the doctor.

The elected assemblyman was Ebenezer Ford, president of the carpenters' union. There were seven write-in votes for Fanny Wright. One person had voted for Benedict Arnold. Another had written in the name of King Ferdinand VII of Spain.

The election of Ford and the large vote cast for the Working Men's candidates frightened the Democrats and the National Republicans. The thought of a common carpenter in the Assembly was a shock to the conservative press. Worse was yet to come, warned the *Journal of Commerce.* The paper argued that it had been a mistake to allow men without property to vote. Imagine "throwing open the polls to every man that walks!"

The *Journal of Commerce* and the other conservative papers need not have worried. The Working Men's Party was soon divided by bitter arguments.

Skidmore attacked editors of the *Free Enquirer* as not representing the working class. Fanny and Dale were rich and educated. They had never worked with their hands. He called for a party "for those, and those only, who lived by the labor of their hands." He set up his own party—the Poor Man's Party—and his own newspaper—the *Friend of Equal Rights.*

He charged Fanny and Dale with genocide for favoring birth control. The *Free Enquirer* articles on population increase were "a crime against society—an attempt to commit the anticipated extinction of the species." He linked them with the writings of Thomas Malthus, the English clergyman who said that poor people ought not to have children if they could not afford to support them. Dale sprang to the defense. "Upon the same principles," he wrote, "bachelors and old maids might be accused of five or six murders apiece."

But it was Fanny's plan for separating children from their parents and educating them in government schools that divided the Working Men's Party. In the important Fifth Ward a public meeting attacked the plan. One worker got up to say that he would not pay taxes to educate other people's children. He preferred to educate his own, and thought everyone else should do the same.

From the *Post* to the *Commercial Advertiser* the papers had a great time fanning the flames of argument within the Working Men's Party. They accused it of trying to break up the family.

Fanny found herself being used as a club to beat the workingmen. She was a hindrance, not a help. Instead of advancing, she was holding back the progress of reform. It would be better for the Working Men's Party and the *Free Enquirer* if she were not on the scene.

Chapter 26 **PARTING OF
THE WAYS**

*Oh, Fanny Wright, sweet Fanny Wright
We ne'er shall hear her more,
She's gone to take another freight
To Hayti's happy shore.*

*For she has gold within her purse,
And brass upon her face;
And talent indescribable,
To give old thoughts new grace.*

*And if you want to raise the wind,
Or breed a moral storm
You must have one bold lady-man
To prate about reform.*

NEW YORK *COURIER
AND ENQUIRER*

IN the back of her mind she worried about the blacks
still at Nashoba. She had promised them their freedom.
But while she ran up and down the cities of the Atlantic
seaboard, lecturing about equality, they slaved away in
the cotton fields of Tennessee.

She knew that conditions had become worse there.
Camilla's baby had died, and she had left her husband
and come to New York. Richesson had stayed behind
to take charge of the property; but he was incapable of

running things. Gilliam, the overseer, had turned brutal and had begun to whip the slaves to make them work. It was clear, despite the wishful dreams of Jefferson and Madison and Monroe, that slavery was not going to disappear of its own accord. In fact, it was becoming more profitable as cotton became the most profitable southern crop. Nashoba was convincing no one.

In the northern states, grudging acceptance of free black people was slowly replaced by hatred. As white workers won political power, they helped to deprive free blacks of their rights. They looked upon black workers as dangerous competitors who might work for lower wages.

In many northern states the white workers who had just won the right to vote supported laws that took that right away from free blacks who owned property. In New Jersey, Pennsylvania, and Connecticut the black right to vote was abolished by law. In New York, the vote was limited to blacks who owned property.

Less than a year after Fanny left Nashoba, the city authorities of Cincinnati ordered all black citizens to leave their homes within thirty days. When black leaders asked for time to find a place to go, white mobs roared through the Negro districts burning houses and attacking black citizens. Between one and two thousand free black Americans had to flee. Most of them went to Canada, where they were welcomed by the royal governor.

In this national atmosphere Fanny felt she must do something about the blacks she had promised to eman-

cipate and colonize. Once more she turned to her old
friend Lafayette. She sent him a letter to forward to
the president of Haiti, Jean Pierre Boyer. She remembered that Boyer had invited George Flower's black
farmers to settle in Haiti when they had to flee Illinois
in 1824.

The president of Haiti accepted Fanny's offer. His
aide Secretary-General Inginiac wrote: "His Excellency
welcomes your desire and offers to all those whose
Haitian blood circulates in their veins an assured refuge . . . . These people in whom you are interested will,
upon landing on our shores, find full and complete freedom."

Boyer also offered to pay the expenses of settling the
American blacks in Haiti.

But who would escort them from Nashoba down the
Mississippi? They could not go alone. Anywhere along
the way they might be captured and sold back into per-
manent slavery.

Fanny was torn between her desire to keep on cam-
paigning for universal state boarding schools and the
Working Men's Party and her own conscience. She
wrote to James Richardson and asked him to take the
blacks to Haiti.

But Richardson was too busy. He and Josephine and
their children were moving to New Orleans. There he
planned to set up a school for free black youngsters. In
this way he would support his family.

Richardson had lost interest in reforming humanity.
He took a pessimistic view of Fanny's efforts to educate
people. He had no great faith in human nature.

"By enlightening the Many," he wrote her, "you will doubtless emancipate them from the tyranny of the Few. But when all are enlightened, what shall prevent the Many from tyrannizing over the Few?"

Robert Jennings was unavailable. He had gone to Boston to help set up a society of free enquirers there. Richesson Whitby flatly said no. Dale had to attend to the daily operation of the *Free Enquirer.* He was also up to his ears in Working Men's Party politics.

She asked Benjamin Lundy to take them. But he had just suffered a death in his family. He declined.

Fanny would have to do the job herself.

At this point William Phiquepal D'Arusmont stepped forward. He had grown bored with printing and proof-reading. He could speak French. He was looking for a chance to get away. He was also looking for a chance to be of help.

Up until now he had admired Fanny from a distance. Dale and Jennings and Richardson and all the others had surrounded her and kept him away. They had put him in the shade with their writing and lecturing. He had been only the teacher, the printer. Now he could be her right arm.

Tall Fanny and short middle-aged D'Arusmont met the slaves and took them to Haiti. There President Boyer gave them land on his own property, providing them, as Fanny later wrote to Lafayette, "with tools, provisions for the first months, and other encouragements free of all charge and rent so long as they choose to remain . . . ."

She and D'Arusmont stayed in the black republic for

six months, long enough to be sure her people were properly settled. Then they returned to the United States.

When they returned, it was clear to Dale and the others that they had become lovers.

In those six months the Working Men's Party had lost ground. Bitter internal arguments had divided it. In Albany, the Democratic legislature had hurriedly passed laws abolishing imprisonment for debt, allocating money to the city's public school, and establishing a mechanic's lien law. That was all many Working Men's Party voters wanted anyway.

Camilla was ill again, physically and emotionally ill. It looked to Fanny like a good time to take a leave of absence. She and Dale agreed she would go to Europe and write articles on European politics for the *Free Enquirer*. Perhaps she would look up Lafayette and other old friends.

"Things move fast in a new world," she told a New York audience at her farewell meeting. "One short year of preparation and the people of this city are already in action. . . ." She referred to the attacks on her, and her wish not to be used as a weapon against the workingman. And then she added: "I shall . . . shortly leave this city and the country for a few months, not to return until after . . . the elections."

In July 1830 she and Camilla were in France. A short time later, D'Arusmont joined them.

VI
Decline and Fall

*After her marriage her charm was bro-
ken and her strength departed from her.*
—ORESTES A. BROWNSON

*I saw but little of Madame D'Arusmont
after her marriage, and lost sight of her
altogether in the latter years of her life.*
—ROBERT DALE OWEN

Chapter 27 MARRIAGE AND MOTHERHOOD

"Poor Frances! I really pity her with all my heart. Is it possible that she would have ended in such a manner? Better if she had drowned herself!"

MME. FRETAGEOT

GUILLAUME Jervis Casimir Phiquepal D'Arusmont—for that was the name he was given at birth—was sixteen years older than Fanny. He preferred to be known as William Phiquepal because it was shorter and sounded more democratic.

He had been a boy of ten when the French Revolution began, and had grown to manhood during years of blood and violence. As a young man he had studied medicine.

He had been a student of the famous French physician Philippe Pinel, the first modern doctor to attempt to treat mentally disturbed patients. Pinel was a pioneer in the humane treatment of the insane, and director of the famous Salpêtrière Asylum for Women. It had been expected that when he retired D'Arusmont would succeed him.

But D'Arusmont had lost interest in medicine. He decided instead to devote his life to the study of education. He became a follower of the Swiss educational reformer Johann Pestalozzi. D'Arusmont's interest in teaching young people useful subjects had led him to New Harmony, and later to Fanny and the *Free Enquirer.*

He was a short, stocky man. When he joined Fanny and Camilla in Paris, he was fifty-one years old. He had thick hair, black mixed with gray, and bushy eyebrows. He was not handsome, but he had strong features and a lively mind.

The little band of reformers, radicals, and free enquirers that had swirled around Fanny in America respected him, but they did not like him. Dale said he was "a suspicious and headstrong man."

"Phiquepal D'Arusmont," he wrote, "[was] a man well informed on many points, full of original ideas, some of practical value, but, withal, a wrong-headed genius."

Orestes A. Brownson, editor of the radical paper *The Sentinel,* said he "never trusted" D'Arusmont.

Walt Whitman was only a boy in his teens when Fanny and her associates were active in New York. When he was a very old man, he remembered D'Arusmont only as "a damned scoundrel."

To Fanny, D'Arusmont was a loyal follower, a true believer. He admired her with great enthusiasm. He went out of his way to do her favors and services. What was most important to her was his dependability.

He had been quick to respond when she needed help in bringing the blacks of Nashoba to Haiti. He was present now in Paris when Camilla was ill. Fanny needed someone to lean on. He took an apartment a few doors down the block from the house in which Fanny and Camilla were living.

He was a great help to the sisters during the turbulent month of July 1830. The people of Paris had exploded in another revolution against their king. There was fighting in the city. Workers and students battled the army and the police. Radical leaders of the workingmen talked of a class war—a war of the poor against the rich. Some of them talked of establishing a system of socialism in which there would be no private property and in which there would be free schools for all.

Fanny thought her time of triumph had come. She sent excited reports back to the *Free Enquirer.*

"What distinguishes the present from every other struggle in which the human race had been engaged," she wrote, "is that the present is . . . a war of class . . . . It is no longer nation pitted against nation for the good pleasure and sport of Kings and great Captains. . . .

". . . It is now everywhere the oppressed millions who are making common cause against their oppressors; it is the ridden people of the earth who are struggling to throw from their backs the 'booted and spurred' riders . . . it is labor rising up against idleness."

But the July Revolution of 1830, as it is called, petered out in four days. The king ran away. The govern-

ment was entrusted to Lafayette. The old man—he was
now seventy-three—was urged by the workers and the
students to declare France a republic.
But he waited and hesitated. He refused to call out
his vast army of supporters. Finally he asked the Duke
of Orlèans, a member of the royal family, if he would
become king. The duke accepted.
France was again a monarchy—with Lafayette's
blessing. The aging hero feared the rule of the people
after all.
Fanny's spirits were crushed. She was disgusted with
her old friend. Things returned to normal: the rich were
still rich; the poor were still poor. Another attempt to
change society had failed.
There were more disappointments. At the end of 1830
Dale wrote from New York that the Working Men's
Party had been unsuccessful in the November elections.
Most workers had voted for the Democratic candidates.
There was no longer a Working Men's Party representa-
tive sitting in the state legislature in Albany.
Fanny had hoped to present her plan for state-sup-
ported boarding schools to the legislature for action.
Now that opportunity was gone. Her great scheme for a
new kind of education was defeated.
In the midst of this defeat and disappointment,
Fanny discovered that she was pregnant. She and D'Ar-
usmont were to have a child.
This must have come as a terrible shock to her. All
her life she had been a free spirit. Now suddenly, at the
age of thirty-five, she had entered the prison of mother-

hood. Nothing in her experience had prepared her psychologically for this traditional feminine role.

She moved into the home of a physician, a friend. His family would care for her during the pregnancy. D'Arusmont stayed at her side.

Camilla, alone and sick, travelled south to escape the bitter Paris winter of 1830–31. Then in February, weaker still, she returned and took an apartment by herself. A few days later she died.

Fanny must have suffered what is now described as a nervous breakdown. She saw no one, wrote to no one. Her friends wrote worried letters, but she did not reply. They wrote to each other, seeking explanations of the sudden change in her. They did not know that she was pregnant.

They wrote to Lafayette for news. He had none. He no longer saw Fanny. She did not write to him, nor did she answer his letters.

D'Arusmont acted as Fanny's strong right arm. He took care of Camilla's funeral arrangements. He witnessed the death certificate. He went back to America to take care of their financial affairs and to settle Camilla's will. She had left some money to Richesson Whitby and some to Robert Dale Owen.

D'Arusmont found the free enquirers on the verge of breaking up. The churches had been defeated in their attempt to compel religious observance, and so the public passion against them had died down. The laws imprisoning debtors had been repealed by Democratic legislators, as workingmen voted for the Democratic party in greater numbers. In their effort to win shorter hours and higher wages, these workingmen began to turn their attention to organizing labor unions. The reform of society did not interest them. Except for a few scattered radical thinkers not very many Americans wanted to make a new world.

Dale still put out the *Free Enquirer,* but the Hall of Science had been sold to a Methodist congregation. The church leaders permitted freethinkers to use it six days each week. On Sundays it was a Methodist Sunday School.

For Fanny, it must have seemed that D'Arusmont was the only human being left to her, now that Camilla was gone. Perhaps she felt drawn to men much older than herself. Lafayette had been her first love. Now D'Arusmont was to be her last. In the years between, she had never seemed able to develop a lasting relationship with younger men.

Neither Fanny nor D'Arusmont believed in marriage. Each believed that one should be able to love another freely, without legal ties, and to leave the other equally freely when an end came to that love.

But after she gave birth to her baby—a girl—she must have realized she could no longer remain free. Perhaps if she had been younger she might have faced the world with an illegitimate child. But this challenge had come too late in her life. She had lost some of her strength.

Some time after the baby was born, on July 22, 1831, Fanny and D'Arusmont were married by an official of the city of Paris. One of the witnesses—the law required two—was Lafayette.

She was Fanny Wright no longer. To the world she was now Mme. D'Arusmont.

On Christmas Day a pioneer member of the New Harmony commune visited Paris. She was Mme. Fretageot, a starchy character and an old acquaintance of Fanny, D'Arusmont, and the other participants in Robert Owen's New Harmony experiment on the banks of the Wabash River.

She stopped in to say Merry Christmas to Lafayette, but the old man was ill. She asked his secretary for Fanny Wright's address.

"Number 8, rue Fréjus," said the secretary.

Mme. Fretageot went there. She asked the concierge for Miss Wright. The woman looked astonished. She had never heard of such a person. Mme. Fretageot went in and walked up the dark stairs of the old house. On the fourth floor she saw light from a half-open door. She knocked at the door.

A young man came to the door. She asked him for Miss Wright, thinking as she did so that he looked familiar. The young man went inside; he came out with a lighted candle, and took her to another door on the same floor. She followed him in.

There was no light in the room except for the candle the young man carried. Mme. Fretageot saw an older man standing in the room. The young man stopped suddenly in front of the older man, and by the light of the candle Mme. Fretageot could see that the older man was Phiquepal D'Arusmont. The young man she now recognized as one of the three boys who had helped D'Arusmont print the *New Harmony Gazette,* and later the *Free Enquirer* in New York.

Both Mme. Fretageot and D'Arusmont started in surprise at the sight of each other. "I had not come to see you," she said. "Where is Miss Wright?"

Neither of the men answered. Madame Fretageot saw a door leading to another room. She went through it. Inside she found a woman who resembled Fanny undressing a baby girl.

"Frances!"

"How did you find my address?" asked the woman.

"I thought you would be glad to see me."

It was indeed Fanny Wright. But a very different person from the Fanny Wright of New Harmony, Nashoba, and New York. She seemed disturbed, carelessly dressed, slow to speak. The starch and fire had gone out of her. "I do not receive visits," she said dully to her old acquaintance.

"I suppose you are too busy writing," said Mme. Fretageot.

"No. I am totally occupied with my family."

Mme. Fretageot asked if she ever visited Lafayette; Fanny said she did not go out. Then Madame asked if it were true, as she had heard in America, that Fanny was writing a biography of the general. Fanny merely said, "Oh."

Mme. Fretageot looked around while Fanny put the baby to bed in the same room. There was an adult bed, a few chairs, a marble-topped stove, a cradle for the baby. It was a shabby, poor, dark room.

"Won't you come and see me?" asked Mme. Fretageot.

"I never go anywhere," said Fanny.

"May I come again to see you?"

There was no answer. Fanny merely looked at her.

"I am sorry if I have disturbed you, Frances," Mme. Fretageot said awkwardly.

The baby began to cry. Fanny went to rock her. Mme. Fretageot prepared to leave. Fanny did not turn around, did not see her to the door, did not say goodbye. Mme. Fretageot stumbled through the dark outer room, banging against chairs and tables. D'Arusmont and the young man had left.

"What does all this mean?" Mme. Fretageot wrote to an old New Harmony friend later. "Is she his wife?" A few days later the mystery was cleared up for her when she met somone who knew them. "Phiquepal has really married Miss Wright," she wrote. "Poor Frances!"

Harriet Garnett also visited Fanny in Paris that winter. "Fanny received me kindly but coldly," she wrote to her sister Julia. "Old friendships, I think, she has forgotten. Old scenes have vanished from her mind. . . . Little Sylva . . . is a fine and I dare say will be a pretty blue-eyed child."

She described Fanny's new life-style. "The muddle is very great. A bedroom, a naked child, Fanny in *robe de*

chambre [bathrobe], a stove and child's victuals cooking—how different from the elegant boudoir in which
we used to find our loved Fanny writing. I thought of
the past . . . and I felt very unhappy."

In April of the following year Fanny gave birth to another daughter. The baby died before it was two months
old.

Chapter 28 A WOMAN'S PLACE

"Fathers and husbands! . . . Do ye not see how, in the mental bondage of your wives and fair companions, ye yourselves are bound?"

FRANCES WRIGHT

FOR Phiquepal D'Arusmont it was all very well to talk of women's rights and of equality between the sexes. The actual experience of marriage and family life was something different.

For years he had admired Fanny's eloquence, wit, learning, and courage. But like most men, he expected his home to revolve around his own needs and interests. He was very much a family man, and he expected his wife to care for his child and do all that was necessary to keep him happy and comfortable.

It was true that Fanny Wright had spoken in public and edited a newspaper. Now she was Mme. D'Arusmont. Respectable married women did not do such things. It would be a reflection on their husbands if they did.

He was considerably older than she, less attractive, less intelligent, had less money. He had published no books, made no speeches, edited no newspapers. He had not chatted with presidents, had not known generals and philosophers. He could hardly claim superior ability to Fanny. Still, he was the man of the family, and therefore by law and custom its absolute ruler.

Fanny tried to be a good wife and mother. But nothing in her life had prepared her for the sudden drudgery of housework at the age of thirty-five. She had spent her life in study, in writing, in lecturing. Now she was confined to a world of diapers, washing, cooking, and scrubbing.

She tried. She submerged herself in the lives of her husband and child. Perhaps if he had been more successful, it would have been easier. But he was impractical and vain, and unable to find a proper means of livelihood. At the age of fifty-three he was still unsure of his future. All his life he had been supported by wealthy reformers.

She ignored the world outside her bedroom and her kitchen and tried to do her duty.

D'Arusmont tried, too. He did more than most men would have done, perhaps because Fanny was often ill. Harriet Garnett visited her again right after the birth of the second baby and reported to her sister Julia: "She was ill. She had no maid with her—her husband brought up the baby by hand—and took charge of the older girl."

The D'Arusmonts lived quietly. They made a few

friends, notably the famous French philosopher Auguste Comte. Then, in 1834, Lafayette died. There is no record of Fanny's reaction.

That year Robert Owen (the elder) invited Fanny to come to England to lecture on education and rational knowledge. Fanny accepted and left her home in Paris. She gave the same lectures she had given since Cincinnati in the summer of 1828. She expounded the same philosophy. Liberal English audiences received her with enthusiasm.

But she was no longer the same free person. D'Arusmont sent her letter after letter from Paris. He told her how much he missed her. He reminded her of Sylva, and told her how much the baby missed her also. He asked in each letter for the date of her return. He recounted endless details of what Sylva ate, what she said, how she felt, and how much she needed her mother.

He was untiring in his efforts to bring her home and keep her home. Once, after nine days passed without a letter, he wrote: "Are you ill? I can't tell you all the evil possibilities which are passing through my head about you." He was a jealous man.

Perhaps Fanny should never have married, should never have become a mother. She found it confining. D'Arusmont, for his part, was insecure and envious. He could never tolerate the slightest freedom for his wife. He was more concerned with the petty details of daily household life than with philosophic and political ideas. In one letter filled with domestic trivia he wrote: "I keep the house cleaner than it has been for a long time."

Fanny did not care. Housecleaning was not her major interest. One radical young carpenter who knew her in Cincinnati wrote, "My wife says she was the most ignorant housekeeper she ever saw, could not sweep a room and do it correctly, could not pack a trunk properly."

In another letter D'Arusmont grew angry at her silence. He insisted that she stop lecturing and come home: "If you are ill you can surely find some means of letting me know. But I am not even sure you are in London . . . . Unless I hear from you before Sunday week, I shall come myself and look for you."

That was just what he did in the end. When he found her, he took her home to Paris. For the time being, she obeyed him.

In 1835 D'Arusmont had to go to America to take care of Fanny's property in Cincinnati. She and Camilla had purchased some real estate there while living in the United States. As her husband, D'Arusmont was legal master of her wealth.

She insisted on going with him. They left three-year-old Sylva with friends and sailed to America on what was to be a short trip—perhaps a few months. In fact, Fanny did not return to Paris and did not see her daughter again for four years.

Once in Cincinnati the magic magnet of the lecture platform pulled Fanny back into her old life. She found the controversy and passion of American political life irresistible. This was her world. This was what she had

always lived for. This had been her destiny since girlhood.

She loved Sylva and often wrote to her. She and
D'Arusmont separated and rejoined each other and separated on and off for the next few years. Many times he
went back to Paris. He tried persistently to get her to
come with him. But he did not succeed.

In those important early years of childhood Sylva
scarcely knew her mother. She never forgave her for this
neglect.

Fanny was fond of D'Arusmont, but she was unable
to be untrue to herself. They exchanged many letters
when they were not together. When they *were* together,
they were irritable and discontented. He never got used
to a wife who was a public figure.

Great issues divided America in 1835. One was slavery, on which Fanny's opinions were well-known. Most
supporters of slavery considered her an abolitionist. In
fact, she was critical of the abolitionists.

The other was the question of allowing the Bank of
the United States to continue to exist.

This private bank, chartered by the federal government, had been the only national bank permitted in the
United States. In the summer of 1832 President Andrew
Jackson had vetoed a renewal of its charter. The bank
would go out of existence in 1836, when its charter ex-
pired—unless a new charter was passed by the Congress
and approved by the President.

Jackson's 1832 veto was very popular. The opposition National Republican party had made it the campaign issue that year—and had been badly beaten. Jackson's victory at the polls was overwhelming. While Fanny and D'Arusmont had been in France, their friends among the radicals, free enquirers, liberals, and Working Men's Party supporters had campaigned for him.

The bank was hated and feared because it had enormous power before it was crippled by Jackson's veto and the subsequent withdrawal of government deposits. It could make or break a businessman by lending or refusing to lend him money. The bank had political power through its corruption of important government officials. Senator Daniel Webster of Massachusetts, for example, received bribes in the form of interest-free loans from the bank.

To the Democratic party and its liberal and radical supporters the Bank of the United States was a government-supported monopoly. They had sworn to destroy all monopolies. The new Whig party championed the bank and threatened to revive it with a new charter if they won the election of 1836.

This time the Democratic candidate for the presidency was Martin Van Buren, Jackson's Vice-President. Fanny's support for Van Buren brought her back to the lecture platform.

She retraced her lecture tour of 1828, beginning in Cincinnati. There she was something of a hometown girl. Her listeners treated her respectfully.

But in Philadelphia a mob tried to break up her meeting. Hoodlums rioted and threw stones that injured members of the audience. The police stood by and did nothing. Fanny called the hoodlums "bank rioters."

She spoke also in New York and Boston. The Democrats supported her wherever she went. In November, Van Buren won, and the bank was dead forever. Fanny was elated. She had found herself again. D'Arusmont left her and returned to France.

Shortly after this she wrote to Sylva, now four: "Dear Child, we imagine ourselves beside you in all your little occupations, your plays, your walks, . . . your visits to the country."

A little later she wrote: "I know, my child, that in no part of the world could you be better off than where you are, surrounded by care and love, and far removed from stupidity, bad example, and bad influences . . . but nevertheless very often . . . tears pour down my cheeks . . . [I] have to remind myself 'How far away she is from me!' "

Fanny settled in Philadelphia and began to edit a new paper, *Manual of American Principles.* She edited and published it by herself. Robert Jennings had disappeared. Robert Dale Owen had married. She and he had nothing more to do with each other.

James Richardson had sent his wife Josephine and their two children to Haiti "where their name [is] no longer nigger." He was a tutor for a rich planter family in Memphis, trying to earn enough money to join them. "I shall follow them," he wrote Fanny with his customary breezy good humor, "whenever the separation shall become intolerable, by which time they will have built a nest and I shall have a few feathers to soften it when I go."

Another old friend from Tennessee, Marcus Winchester, had married a black woman. He was rich and prominent, but he too suffered from American racism. He worried about his children's future, about their happiness and their safety.

Fanny still felt that the problem of race in America could only be solved by the mixture of the races. But it was not safe even to talk about that. "At the present time," she wrote Winchester, "the least said on the subject the better."

Slavery and race had become the leading political issue. It was tearing the country apart. The gentle old abolitionists like Benjamin Lundy had been succeeded by fire-eating idealists like William Lloyd Garrison. A black slave named Nat Turner had led a bloody insurrection in Virginia that had frightened the wits out of southern whites. Jefferson and Madison and Monroe had been succeeded by violent militants like John Calhoun, who would rather see the Union destroyed than slavery ended.

America was becoming violent and irrational over the question of slavery. Garrison was almost lynched by a proslavery mob in Boston. Abolitionist editors and speakers were beaten, murdered, and shouted down all across the country. Well-dressed mobs threw stones at Quaker preachers. The year Fanny campaigned for Van

Buren, Congress adopted a "gag rule" which forbade any discussion of slavery.

The Democrats supported, apologized for, and defended slavery. The Whigs, especially the northern Whigs, were less friendly to slavery. Most of the old workingmen radicals hated the abolitionists for their political and economic conservatism. Some supported slavery out of racism. Fanny herself, while opposing slavery, disliked the abolitionists because they were religious.

She was over forty now. It was a new time. Events had overtaken her. Whigs attacked her for opposing the bank and for opposing their conservative economic measures. Democrats were suspicious of her antislavery views. She was abused and insulted in the press of both parties.

In 1838 she campaigned for the Democrats in the congressional elections. In New York a mob shouted her down. Someone yelled, "Put her out! Put the old bitch out!"

She had not lost her old coolness. Amos Gilbert, a Quaker friend who edited the *Free Enquirer* in the thirties, described her behavior under such fire:

"After the platform on which she held forth was demolished, she has been seen descending from the second story of a building after she had finished a lecture, with thousands of grim faces peering upon her, giving savage indications of murderous intent, so soon as their masters should give the word 'go.' But her calm intre-

pidity awed them, and she was permitted to pass
through the formidable crowd to the carriage un-
scathed.

"When she was ensconced out of sight in the vehicle
—when her tranquil firmness was invisible to them—
they several times lifted and leaned the carriage, trying
themselves, whether they had the audacious courage to
throw it over. Prudent, resolute men walked slowly before the horses, repeating 'steady, steady' . . . Meantime Frances sat gently fanning herself, and in easy conversation with her friends."

Former President Andrew Jackson attacked her when
he learned that her opposition to slavery was hurting the
Democrats. When he heard she had lectured in Washington, he wrote to a friend that all her efforts could accomplish would be to divide the party. "She may do
harm," he said, "but can do no good."

A year later the *Colored American* attacked her for
not knowing her place as a woman. "Fanny Wright's
first steps toward skepticism," it said, "were her masculine assumptions. Male speculations and male achieve-
ments engrossed her soul. The fatal result was to be expected—she is now a leader in *masculine infidelity*—one
of the grossest skeptical disorganizers that ever cursed
the world.

"Ladies are *lovely, truly lovely* in their place, but alas!
when they abandon it!"

Chapter 29 DIVORCE AND
DEATH

*"I ask nothing more from you but to give up the
deed to the Tennessee property . . . and to with-
draw your suit."*

M. D'ARUSMONT TO
FRANCES WRIGHT D'ARUSMONT

FANNY took no more part in the growing women's rights
movement than she did in the abolitionist movement. In
the 1840's she had come to feel that only a thorough-
going change in the whole structure of society could accomplish individual reforms. Changes in the rights of
women, of blacks, and of working people, she said,
would have to wait upon the great master change of all:
the creation of a new society based on a kind of socialism. In such a perfect world men and women would
work because they wanted to, not because they were
forced to in order to feed themselves and their families.
Every person would be cared for in accordance with his
or her need.

She lived mostly in Cincinnati now, when she was not
traveling. D'Arusmont and Sylva lived in Paris and cor-

responded with her. He traveled back and forth, and they met occasionally, but they no longer lived together as man and wife. Sylva was growing up, as Fanny had, without a mother.

Fanny had been deprived of her mother by death; Sylva was neglected. Fanny found the lecture platform more exciting and more satisfying than being a wife and mother. She would have liked both D'Arusmont and Sylva to travel with her and attend all her meetings. She wanted Sylva to follow her path in life and become a public speaker and reformer. But the girl disliked public meetings and showed no interest in politics, and her father encouraged her in this.

In one of his more bitter later letters, D'Arusmont wrote, looking back on their unhappy marriage: "Your husband and child ranked only as mere appendages to your personal existence."

In Cincinnati in the early 1840's a group of bright young workingmen organized a club called the Franklin Institute. They hoped to create something like the old New York Hall of Science. In the Franklin Institute the young mechanics organized courses and lecture series to improve their education.

Every Wednesday night there were debates. On Sundays, instead of going to church, they came to their club room and listened to a lecture. Often they invited Fanny to speak to them. She lent them books and gave them copies of her lectures of the past.

At the club she met a radical young carpenter, Joel

Brown. He became a great friend of Fanny's and of D'Arusmont's when he was in Cincinnati. When the time came for Fanny to have her house built, she asked Joel to do the job.

"I want this clay building taken down," she said to him, "and a brick house erected in its place. What will it cost, considering that I want the house to be the same size, with the same number of rooms?"

Young Brown said it would cost two thousand dollars. She told him to go ahead and do the job.

"After the building was partly enclosed," Brown remembered years later, "I moved my work bench into it."

To his astonishment Fanny moved in a few days later. She brought with her a charcoal furnace, a few chairs, a table, a writing desk, and some kitchen utensils. The house was barely livable, but still she moved in. "Her food consisted of boiled beef, eggs, potatoes, crackers, and tea or coffee," said Brown. "She was a plain liver.

"I did not like her moving into the house. I thought her object was to get more work out of us. But I found I was mistaken. She hindered us, with her theories for the advancement of working men."

Brown and the masons, plasterers, and other workers he hired to do the job were fascinated by Fanny's method of preparing a lecture. "She would write a few sentences, then get up and walk whispering to herself, repeating what she had written."

If Joel Brown's memory is to be trusted Fanny was a

perceptive prophet. For she told him and his fellow workers what she thought the United States would be like in the coming half century. And much of what she predicted came true.

"In fifty years," Brown remembers her saying, "the whole United States would be literally covered with railroads; cities would spring up in every quarter of the country; the capitalists would grab up all the land; it would be difficult for a working man to get a home . . . the center of railroad traffic would be in New York and other large cities, creating millionaires by the score . . . millionaires are a dangerous class . . . [they] will control the politics of the United States."

This is an astonishingly accurate prediction. Fifty years after she made it, in the 1890's, the Populist party used almost the same words in their speeches and pamphlets attacking the political power of "Wall Street."

Her pessimism about the future may have been a reflection of her sadness and loneliness. Sylva was growing up estranged from her. D'Arusmont had won the girl's heart.

Then, in 1844, a letter came from the British Embassy in Washington. Her father's cousin Margaret had died. This left Fanny the only living member of the Wright family and the heir to all the wealth and property accumulated by her grandfather Alexander Wright. She was an extremely rich woman.

She went to Dundee to settle the legal details of her inheritance. While she was there, she worked on her last book, *England the Civilizer.* Then she went to Paris to stay with D'Arusmont and Sylva. She wanted very much to be with her family. Sylva, now twelve, had written her a long and loving letter, filled with little endearments about her "beloved little Mommy" and of how wonderful it would be "on that day when the three of us are together again." She signed the letter "your daughter who loves you and will always love you."

But D'Arusmont was even more bitter now that Fanny was very wealthy again. He was an old man. He had never earned a living. What would happen if Fanny took all her wealth and abandoned him?

He asked her to sign an agreement putting all her property in Sylva's name in case she died, and providing also that as long as he lived he would have a sufficient income. She did so. But it was not enough to reassure him.

When it became apparent that Fanny could not live with him and she returned to Cincinnati, he worried. He heard rumors that she was interested in new schemes for the emancipation of the slaves. Perhaps she would spend all her money on a new Nashoba? Or on a new *Free Enquirer*?

In the end Fanny had to bring suit for divorce. In the United States at that time this was the only way a married woman could regain control of her property. When D'Arusmont heard that she was suing him, he wrote her a long, self-pitying letter in which he mixed threats with his insistence that he truly loved her. He described himself as "a man of simple habits, devoted to truth and justice," and "a lover of liberty." "Of what use is a divorce?" he asked pleadingly, since he was sure she did not expect to marry anyone else. He begged her to give up her control of the property in Tennessee, the Nashoba lands, and to abandon her suit for divorce.

Finally he threatened her. "If it is war and not peace you desire you will find me ready to defend our rights. . . . This letter, Frances, is . . . neither a prayer nor a menace; it is a last and friendly warning." With the letter, which he mailed on October 1, 1850, D'Arusmont included a stern note from the American consul in Paris offering the opinion that Fanny would be better off if she stopped her legal action and ended all "domestic feuds."

But Fanny continued her suit, and despite D'Arusmont's threats, she won her divorce. Immediately after that, she won her case in a Cincinnati court for the return of full control over her property.

It was a sad, bitter, empty victory. She was fifty-five; he was seventy-one. She had hoped that after it was all over she and Sylva would be able to love one another. A meeting was arranged by Fanny's lawyer. But it was a failure. Sylva was bitter and supported her father.

A few months later, Fanny fell on the ice in her front yard and broke her hip. She lay in bed all through 1852 in great pain. She did not heal.

On Monday morning, December 13, 1852, "being," she said, "of sound mind and memory, but very ill and not long to live," she made her will. She left small sums to various friends and to her lawyer. "I give the rest of my property," she wrote, "to my daughter Frances

Sylva D'Arusmont, who has been alienated from me, but to whom, with said property, I give my blessing and forgiveness for the sorrows she has caused her mother."

Then she died.

Chapter 30 UNFULFILLED DREAM

". . . without regard to sex or condition, class, race, nation, or color . . . ."
FRANCES WRIGHT,
NOTES ON NASHOBA

SHE was buried in Spring Grove Cemetery, in Cincinnati. The world took little notice: a few lines in the *Cincinnati Gazette,* a rather longer obituary in *The New York Daily Times.*

A little more than twenty years after Fanny's death, her daughter Sylva, now a middle-aged married woman with two sons, testified before the Committee of the Judiciary of the House of Representatives. This committee was considering the request that women living in Washington, D.C., be permitted to vote. Mrs. Guthrie—for that was her name—was opposed to giving women this right.

"She held that the ballot in the hands of woman would demoralize society, undermine the state, and tend to detract from the finer qualities of the sex, and consequently destroy her usefulness as a mother, wife, and citizen," a Washington newspaper reported.

The paper noted that Mrs. Guthrie thanked the congressional committee for permitting her to testify. When she had tried to speak earlier at a woman-suffrage meeting in Lincoln Hall, she had been denied the floor.

Some years after Sylva advised Congress not to give women the vote, Susan B. Anthony and her sister women's-rights leaders wrote *A History of Woman's Suffrage.* On the title page of the first volume the dedication reads: "Affectionately inscribed to the memory of Mary Wollstonecraft, [and] Frances Wright. . . ." Opposite the title page is an engraved portrait of Fanny. It is the only picture in the book.

A few years later, Walt Whitman, now an old man and the most famous poet in America, remembered his boyhood in New York City and the times his father had taken him to the Hall of Science and he had seen Frances Wright. "We all loved her; fell down before her; her very appearance seemed to enthrall us. . . . she was more than beautiful; she was grand! It was not feature simply but soul—soul. There was a majesty about her."

In her *Explanatory Notes on Nashoba* she had written of her dream: "To develop all the intellectual and physical powers of all human beings, without regard to sex or condition, class, race, nation or color . . . ."

Still an unfulfilled dream . . .

*Quotations from the Writings
of Frances Wright*

"I do not see any prospect of reform . . . until a new generation shall be raised . . . until children shall be protected (alike) from the errors and the ignorance, the vices and misfortunes of their parents . . . ."
—*Free Enquirer,* JULY 22, 1829

"Our teachers . . . are compelled to administer to our prejudices and to perpetuate our ignorance. They dare not speak that which by endangering their popularity would endanger their fortunes. They have to discover not what is true but what is palatable . . . ."
—*Free Enquirer,* JANUARY 14, 1829

"[Men] are incomprehensible animals . . . . They walk about boasting of their wisdom, strength, and sovereignty, while they have not sense so much as to swallow an apple without the aid of an Eve to put it down their throats."
—LETTER TO MARY SHELLEY, MARCH 20, 1828

"Fathers and husbands! . . . Do ye not see how, in the mental bondage of your wives and fair companions, ye yourselves are bound?"

—LECTURE ON KNOWLEDGE

"Many, of course, think me mad, and if to be mad means to be one of a minority I am so, and very mad indeed, for our minority is very small."

—LETTER TO MARY SHELLEY, SEPTEMBER 29, 1827

"I am no Christian, in the sense usually attached to that word. I am neither Jew nor Gentile, Mohammedan or Theist. I am but a member of the human family."

—LECTURE IN CINCINNATI, 1828

"I conceive the marriage contract, as by law existing, to deprive the female of all defence, by abrogating all her natural rights as a human being, and all her artificial rights as a citizen."

—*New Harmony Gazette*, 1828

"[May] the olive of peace and brotherhood be embraced by the white man and the black, and their children, approached in feeling and education, gradually blend into one their blood and their hue."
"False opinion and vicious institutions have perverted the best source of human happiness—the intercourse of the sexes—into the deepest source of human misery."

—*Explanatory Notes on Nashoba*, 1827

Bibliography

THERE are only two full-length biographies of Frances Wright, and both of them are out of print: William Randall Waterman, *Frances Wright*, New York, 1924, is scholarly and authoritative; A. J. G. Perkins and Theresa Wolfson, *Frances Wright, Free Enquirer*, New York, 1939, is gossipy and popular in tone. It is not annotated and is inaccurate in many details. Both biographies rely on manuscript material no longer available.

Two short biographic sketches are Amos Gilbert, *Memoir of Frances Wright*, Cincinnati, 1855, a brief and often shallow reminiscence by one of her editors; and the manuscript memoir of Joel Brown, set down many years after her death (Public Library of Cincinnati and Hamilton County). As a young radical Cincinnati carpenter, Joel Brown knew Frances Wright personally, built her house, and followed her political leadership. He reports her own account of her early life.

The major source about that early life is her own third-person autobiography, *Biography, Notes, and Political Letters of Frances Wright D'Arusmont*, New York, 1844. An important source by a close friend and collaborator is Robert Dale Owen, *Twenty-Seven Years of Autobiography*, published in installments in the *Atlantic Monthly*, January–November, 1873, and also "An Earnest Sowing of Wild Oats," in the *Atlantic Monthly*, July 1874. First-hand observations and recollections and personal impressions of her husband are to be found in Orestes A. Brownson, *The Convert*, New York, 1857. Frances Wright and Nashoba are seen through the perceptive (and somewhat critical) eyes of Frances Trollope in her *Domestic Manners of the Americans*, London, 1832. Horace Traubel, *With Walt Whitman in Camden*, New York, 1905–1912, offers a thumbnail sketch by a passionate admirer; this may be balanced by the acid view of Bernard Eisenach, Duke of Saxe-Weimar, *Travels Through North America During the Years 1825 and 1826*, Philadelphia, 1828.

Other thumbnail sketches of the woman and her ideas are to be found in the letters of Albert Gallatin (New-York Historical Society), James Madison, and the Marquis de Lafayette (Historical Society of Pennsylvania) (Library of the University of Chicago), Mary Shelley (British Museum), Thomas Jefferson (*Thomas Jefferson Correspondence*, Bixby Collection, Boston, 1916) (*Basic Writings of Thomas Jefferson*, Philip S. Foner, New York, 1944), and Andrew Jackson (*Bulletin of the Histor-*

ical and Philosophical Society of Ohio, Cincinnati, January 1958).

Much of Frances Wright's thinking is expressed in her published writings. Her early view of the world and of the United States is found in her famous volume of travel letters, *Views of Society and Manners in America*, London, 1821. A new edition edited by Professor Paul R. Baker, Cambridge, Mass., 1963, has an excellent and well-documented introduction and brief biography.

For an understanding of the thinking that lay behind her maturer views on slavery, race, women's rights, and the utopian reordering of society, a reading of three basic documents written by Frances Wright is essential. These are *A Plan for the Gradual Abolition of Slavery in the United States Without Danger of Loss to the Citizens of the South*, published in the *New Harmony Gazette*, October 1, 1825; *Explanatory Notes, Respecting the Nature and Objects of the Institution of Nashoba*, in the *New Harmony Gazette*, January 30, 1828; and the *Deed to the Lands of Nashoba, West Tennessee*, collection of the Public Library of Cincinnati and Hamilton County. Her letters to Harriet and Julia Garnett (private collection of Cecilia Payne Gaposchkin) also contain much important information concerning the development of her utopian ideas.

Almost all her public lectures, many of her letters and articles, and her writings on the various causes that attracted her interest are to be found in the *Free Enquirer*, New York, 1828–1830. Others are in that paper's predecessors, the *New Harmony Gazette* and the *New Har-*

mony and Nashoba Gazette, New Harmony, Indiana. Her most important lectures are also in *Course of Popular Lectures*, New York, 1829. Other political writings are in *An Address to the Industrious Classes* . . . , New York, 1830, and *What is the Matter?*, New York, 1838.

Other books by Frances Wright are the play *Altorf,* Philadelphia, 1819; *A Few Days in Athens*, London, 1822; and *England the Civilizer*, London, 1848.

Contemporary newspaper accounts are important sources of information about the nature of life in America that led to the rise of the free enquirers and other radicals and the Working Men's Party. These include the *Evening Post*, the *Commercial Advertiser*, the *Courier and Enquirer*, the *New York American*—all of New York—and the *Cincinnati Chronicle*. Of special importance is *The Working Man's Advocate*, New York, 1829–1831, one of the country's earliest labor newspapers. Other special publications of value are Benjamin Lundy's abolitionist *The Genius of Universal Emancipation* and the New York free-thought paper *The Correspondent*.

For a general survey of working conditions in the 1820's and 1830's see John R. Commons, *et al., History of Labor in the United States*, New York, 1918, and Philip S. Foner, *History of the Labor Movement in the United States*, New York, 1947. For details of life in New York before and during Frances Wright's first visit see *The Memorial History of the City of New York*, edited by James Grant Wilson, New York, 1893. Issues of the New York newspapers listed above and of the *New*

York Columbian for the years 1818 and 1819 add much
to that picture, including reports of the reactions to the
production of *Altorf.* An excellent survey of the Jack-
sonian period, of which Frances Wright was both a her-
ald and a principal actor, is to be found in Arthur M.
Schlesinger, Jr., *The Age of Jackson,* Boston, 1945.

Frances Wright said little about the free black population and their problems. Yet blacks were an important
element of the political scene in New York and other
northern cities in the 1820's and 1830's. For information
about what blacks said and thought (and about what
they did *not* say and think) see James Weldon Johnson,
Black Manhattan, New York, 1968 (paper); Roi Ottley
and William J. Weatherby, *The Negro in New York,*
New York, 1969; and Leon F. Litwack, *North of
Slavery,* Chicago, 1961. *The Rights of All,* New York, a
black newspaper published by Samuel E. Cornish, con-
tains commentary on the question of emancipation and
subsequent colonization in Africa or Haiti. Five issues
of this newspaper, all of the year 1829, are in the
Schomburg Collection, New York City.

For fragmentary insights into the circumstances of
Frances Wright's last years, divorce, and death, see letter from Sylva D'Arusmont, February 15, 1845; letter
from Phiquepal D'Arusmont, October 1, 1850; and the
last will of Frances Wright, December 13, 1852—all in
the collection of the Cincinnati Historical Society.
There is an incomplete copy of the pretrial divorce pro-
ceeding at the Paris Consulate of the United States,
April 25, 1848, in the Wright Papers, Library of Con-

gress. A report of the final trial is in the *Daily Commercial*, Cincinnati, August 5, 1851. There are obituaries in the *Cincinnati Daily Gazette*, December 15, 1852, and the *New York Daily Times*, December 18, 1852.

Index

About the Author

Richard Stiller was born and raised in New York City and educated at New York University and Teachers College, Columbia University. He taught history for ten years in New York City and Miami, Florida, high schools before he turned to writing. He is the author of two novels, *The Best Policy* and *The Felix Factor*; of *Broken Promises: The Strange History of the Fourteenth Amendment*; and of *Queen of Populists: The Story of Mary Elizabeth Lease*, an earlier biography in the Women of America series.

Mr. Stiller writes on medical subjects; he and his wife, together with their son and daughter, live in Mount Vernon, New York.